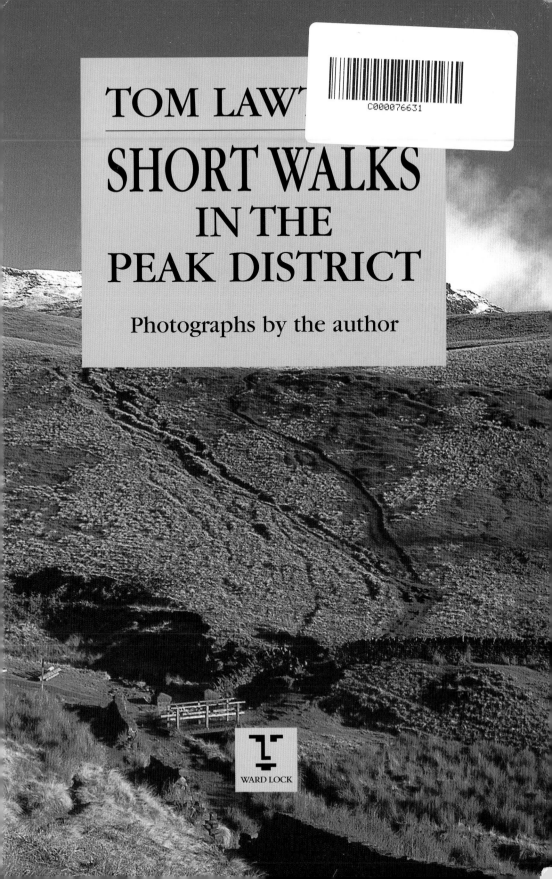

TOM LAWT

SHORT WALKS
IN THE
PEAK DISTRICT

Photographs by the author

WARD LOCK

To Bob Carter, Eddie Fiddler, Bill Rouse, Chris Sennitt and many other walking companions, both individuals and groups, who have contributed greatly and over many years to making my explorations of the Peak District such a joyous adventure.

A WARD LOCK BOOK

First published in the UK 1998
by Ward Lock
Wellington House
125 Strand
LONDON
WC2R OBB

A Cassell Imprint
Copyright © Tom Lawton 1998

The maps in this book were prepared from Harvey Walker's Maps or out-of-copyright Ordnance Survey material. Copyright reserved Harvey Maps 1998.

Distributed in the United States
by Sterling Publishing Co., Inc.
387 Park Avenue South, New York, NY 10016–8810

A British Library Cataloguing in Publication Data block for this book may be obtained from the British Library

ISBN 0 7063 7580 7

Design and page make-up by Chris Bell
Printed and bound in Slovenia by arrangement with Korotan d.o.o., Ljubilana

Frontispiece: *Below the western edges of Kinder Scout.*

CONTENTS

PREFACE

WALKING is both a form of exercise and a way to relax. In fact, it is generally accepted that walking is one of the healthiest of exercises and, if undertaken regularly, will make a significant contribution to physical fitness, while walking through areas of outstanding natural beauty, admiring the scenery and listening to birds singing and to the sound of moving water, is a very good way of relaxing, away from the pressures of modern life. Happily, walking is an exercise which may be pursued by people of all ages, of most shapes and sizes, and at virtually any starting level of fitness and physical capability. In addition, in the case of the short walks described in this book, only relatively modest periods of time need to be set aside to undertake an enjoyable activity which is also inherently good for you.

Reflections in Ladybower Reservoir.

Fortunately, the landscapes of the British Isles provide a number of beautiful and extensive walking areas, many lying conveniently close to heavily populated conurbations. The National Parks were in fact designated to preserve this precious natural heritage and to make these areas generally accessible to the public. Walking through them has become an exceptionally popular pastime, generating a mixture of enjoyment, interest, fulfilment, a sense of achievement, a closeness with nature, a better understanding of the landscape and its evolution, and a general feeling of well-being. We have also become healthier – both mentally and physically – as we walk!

The Peak National Park in particular, has much to offer walkers, including those keen on tackling short routes. The first reason for this is its unique, weathered topography, where the high, exposed acid moorlands, gritstone edges and tors, intermingled sandstones and shales of the Dark Peak partly encircle the pearly-white gorges and dales and the lush green hillsides of the White Peak, which is situated on carboniferous limestone. Where else can you find such walker-friendly landscapes gathered together in such a compact and accessible area? In addition to its obvious scenic beauty, the second attribute of the Peak District is the multitude of places and features of interest to be discovered and explored on foot within its boundaries. Examples include such places as Peveril Castle, numerous caverns and mines with stalactites and stalagmites, Lyme Hall, Errwood Hall, Lud's Church, Chatsworth House, Haddon Hall and numerous remains of ancient settlements and of our industrial heritage, but there are many more.

For these compelling reasons, this book presents a collection of short walks in the Peak District. This selection includes several popular and well-known routes, as well as a number of much less frequented trails and paths. Many of the walks incorporate features of interest and fascinating places to visit. Each walk is described in detail and illustrated with colour photographs and innovative diagrams. My hope is that this collection of routes, and the way in which it is presented, will provide further purpose and inspiration to those who have already trod these ways, as well as an irresistible incentive for others to do the same. Should these hopes be realized, my endeavours will have been well rewarded.

Tom Lawton

ACKNOWLEDGMENTS

Once again, it gives me pleasure to record my gratitude to the many kind people who have contributed to the completion of yet another of my books. They have once more given generously of their leisure time and expertise to make this walking guide possible. To all of you, please accept my warm appreciation and sincere thanks for your efforts, and for the generous way in which you undertook them.

My special thanks are due to several friends and walking companions who accompanied me on the walks and/or contributed in other ways. In particular, I would like to thank Bob Carter for his vast knowledge of and empathy with the Peak District; and Eddie Fidler, who, with Bob, meticulously checked my draft manuscript and audited the proof stages of the book so professionally.

I again talked to any fellow walker who would stop and talk to me while out and about, and these exchanges of views and experiences between people who share a common bond once again stimulated my endeavours and gave further purpose and direction to my efforts. Their continued comments and helpful suggestions are much appreciated, and are reflected in my writings.

Finally, may I once again express my thanks and gratitude for their cheerful support to my wife Bridget and two daughters Katrina and Helen, who continue to accept my many forays into high places and the subsequent time I spend endeavouring to record these accurately.

Some fantastic snow shapes on Dale Top.

WALK LOCATIONS

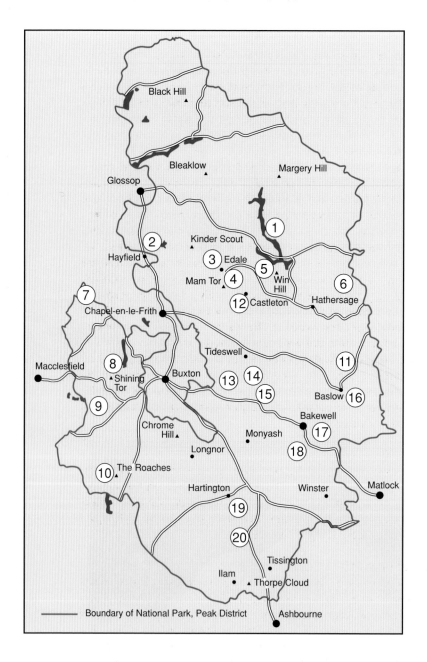

USING THE BOOK

THIS book covers a series of varied short walks in the Peak National Park. Because there are numerous places of interest in the area, wherever possible the walks have been incorporated into wider explorations which provide opportunities to visit these attractions. All in all, there should be something for everyone!

THE ROUTES
The route descriptions cover 20 walks in detail, spread over the differing landscapes of both the millstone grits and acid moorlands of the Dark Peak and the carboniferous limestone of the White Peak. In making this selection, care has been taken to include a range of walks which vary from easy strolls along sheltered dales or by the side of protected reservoirs, to routes that penetrate the higher, more exposed moorlands and tors, and sometimes involve a relatively energetic ascent to the summit of a modestly sized hill. The difficult, exposed, remote and relatively dangerous peat hags and boggy terrain of Black Hill, Bleaklow Head and Kinder Scout have been deliberately avoided. The walks are circular and they all start and finish at a conveniently located carpark or layby. The description of each walk covers the entire route in detail, pointing out features of interest, as well as any potential hazards, along the way. Maps and diagrams are provided for each walk, along with superb colour photographs giving just a taste of the landscapes you will encounter.

WALK DETAILS
Each route description begins with an information summary, including amenities, which will help you to decide on the suitability of the particular walk for you and your party. The main points are themselves summarized in the table on page 158, providing an at-a-glance reference to all 20 routes.

GRADING OF WALKS
The time of the year, the weather and ground conditions, the walkers' ages, physical condition, walking ability and experience, and their knowledge of the area will all affect their appraisal of how difficult they may find a specific walk on a particular day. Nevertheless, and bearing in mind that all the routes are considered 'short', each walk has been graded as either 'easy/straightforward' or 'moderate/challenging'.

Easy/straightforward These walks are for the most part along fairly level ground, with no sustained severe or difficult uphill slopes. Where some modest climbs are involved, these are well spaced out and not unduly strenuous. There is no potentially dangerous exposure or difficult terrain of any consequence, and the walk covers the minimum of waterlogged ground and few boggy areas. Route finding presents limited problems on these walks and the way is nearly always adequately signed. Paths are mostly clear and good, and the greater part of the route is along these. The walks are frequently suitable for family groups with, more often than not, plenty of general interest in addition to the surrounding views and landscapes.

Moderate/challenging These walks remain suitable for all reasonably fit walkers who wish to follow a route which could occupy a good half to full day spent among the dales and moors. However, they do include a combination of features which makes them more exacting than the other category: perhaps some sustained or energetic climbing, together with a longer, more complicated route, sections of which are not as clearly defined as might be expected. On occasion these routes will not be confined to clearly defined footpaths but will involve some walking across open moorland to provide a taste of more adventurous walking (this is noted in the descriptions of the few walks where it applies). This category of walks is less suitable for younger children but should appeal to stronger, older, adventurous youngsters accompanied by experienced adults.

TIME ALLOWANCE

Estimates of walking time have been provided for each route, excluding any allowances for stops such as coffee breaks, lunch and taking photographs. The estimates are generous and have been calculated by allowing 1 hour to walk each 3km (almost 2 miles) and a further half an hour for each 250m (750ft) climbed, with a final adjustment of up to plus or minus half an hour per walk, depending upon additional factors such as ease or difficulty of route finding, state of the paths, type of terrain and so on. You can adjust these basic estimates to suit your own walking speed.

TACKLING THE WALK

At the end of the detailed route description, advice is provided on the appeal and/or adaptability of the walk for three categories: casual walkers, family walkers and strong, experienced walkers. Although there will be some overlap between these, most walkers should be able to place themselves and their party in the relevant category fairly easily. The comments given under the three headings will provide you with some indication of what to expect and how to organize the walk so that everyone taking part will enjoy it to the full.

PLACES OF INTEREST

Finally, brief details are provided on places of interest which are either incorporated into the walking route or may conveniently be visited while in the vicinity. Contact addresses and telephone numbers for these are listed in the Useful Addresses and Publications section (see pages 153-6).

The limestone cliffs of Chee Dale.

11

ABBREVIATIONS

The minimum number of abbreviations has been used, and only to avoid constant repetition.

L	left	NW	north west
R	right	NNW	north north west
N	north	cm	centimetre(s)
NNE	north north east	ft	foot/feet
NE	north east	km	kilometre(s)
ENE	east north east	m	metre(s)
E	east	yd	yard(s)
ESE	east south east	G-stile	gap stile (squeezer stile)
SE	south east	L-stile	ladder stile
SSE	south south east	P-stile	post stile
S	south	S-stile	step stile
SSW	south south west	W-stile	wall stile
SW	south west	K-gate	kissing gate
WSW	west south west	MR	map reference
W	west	OLM(s)	Outdoor Leisure Map(s)
WNW	west north west	OS	Ordnance Survey

DIAGRAMS

A diagram is provided for each route, which gives both a plan and a cross-sectional relief of the walk. These diagrams are based upon grid reference points downloaded from Harvey Maps or from out-of-copyright Ordnance Survey Maps in the Outdoor Leisure Series 1:25 000; 4cm to 1km (2½in to 1 mile). The relief cross section is mathematically integral with the plan and accurately follows the line of the route.

MAPS AND MISCELLANEOUS

Route finding In addition to the maps and route description provided in this book, you should use the Ordnance Survey Outdoor Leisure Maps and a reliable compass at all times when you are walking in the Peak District, even on these short walks. Be sure that you are able to use this combination correctly. Get into the habit of knowing where you are all the time, for some multiple path intersections on lower ground, especially in forested areas or in enclosed landscapes, can be confusing, while on the higher, open moorlands mist and cloud can blow in very quickly indeed, seriously restricting distant vision.

The Ordnance Survey Maps are excellent but not infallible. On the rare occasions where there are differences between the route descriptions and the paths shown on the OS maps (or not shown, as the case may be), rely on the route descriptions in this book

12

In addition, the man-made features of the Peak District are constantly changing: fences appear and disappear, κ-gates replace ʟ-stiles and vice versa, additional waymarker signs appear and others are removed. Should you come across isolated differences along the route from those described, presume that these have occurred since the book went to press, and proceed with confidence to the next certain feature described.

Compass bearings All compass bearings have been given to the nearest 22½ degree point, eg (N), (NNE), (NE) etc. This is considered to be sufficiently accurate over the relatively small distances travelled between the taking of successive readings. Take confirmatory compass bearings as necessary, particularly when the visibility is poor and/or you may become unsure of your exact position.

Heights The heights of the major hills have been given in both metric and imperial measurements. The metric heights have been extracted from the relevant, up-to-date Ordnance Survey Maps. The imperial equivalents have been calculated from these by using a conversion factor of 0.3048m to 1ft. These equivalents have then been rounded-off to the nearest 5ft.

Spelling Sometimes there is more than one version of the spelling of place names. In such instances the spelling which appears on the Ordnance Survey Outdoor Leisure Maps has been used, unless otherwise indicated. There are apparent anomalies which are justified, eg 'Mill Dale' (the valley) and 'Milldale' (the hamlet).

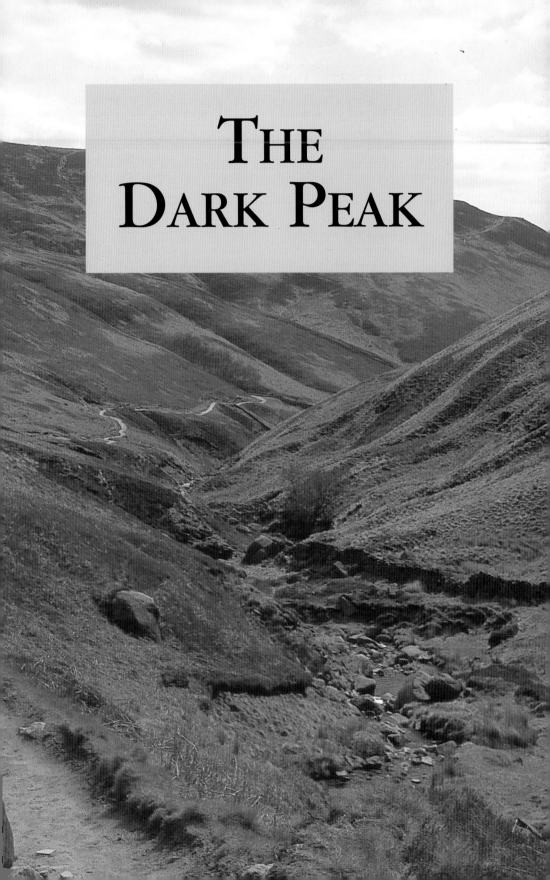

THE
DARK PEAK

1 DERWENT RESERVOIR AND THE UPPER DERWENT VALLEY

**STARTING/
FINISHING POINT**
Carpark at
Fairholmes Visitor
Centre OLM 1:
MR 173893

**GRADING
OF WALK**
Easy/straight-
forward

**TIME
ALLOWANCE**
3 hours

DISTANCE
7.2km (4.5 miles)

**TOTAL HEIGHT
GAINED**
225m (740ft)

HIGHEST POINT
Near Bamford House
380m (1245ft)

GRADIENTS
Just one gradual climb away from the reservoir and a similar descent back to lower ground.

PARKING
Large, well-appointed carpark that is screened by trees, with separate parking bays.

PUBLIC TRANSPORT
Bus routes 257, 274, 395, 400, 460, 795, 796 and BB1.

OVERVIEW/INTEREST
Magnificent forest and moorland scenery surrounding reservoirs. Features massive dam walls. Plenty of wildlife – particularly birds, including waterfowl. Sheltered picnic spots and open landscapes. Association with the famous 'Dambusters'.

AMENITIES
Light refreshments and toilets, including facilities for the disabled, at Fairholmes Visitor Centre. Information point and Ranger Service operate from here. Cycles for hire from the Peak National Park Centre also located here.

FOOTPATHS AND WAYSIGNS
Service roads, trails and footpaths are good to excellent for most of the way. Climb up and descent are along rougher, narrower paths. Plentiful waysigns are extremely helpful.

Previous pages:
The long trail up
Grindsbrook.

WALK back past the information/toilet block and then bear R along the footpath signed 'Footpath: to Derwent Dam', heading N. Veer R again when you reach the service road ahead and walk towards Derwent Dam, crossing over a connecting stream on your way. The massive dam, with its two castellated towers, will soon come into view, high above on your L. The lane then swings around gradually to the R and you must spot and use the

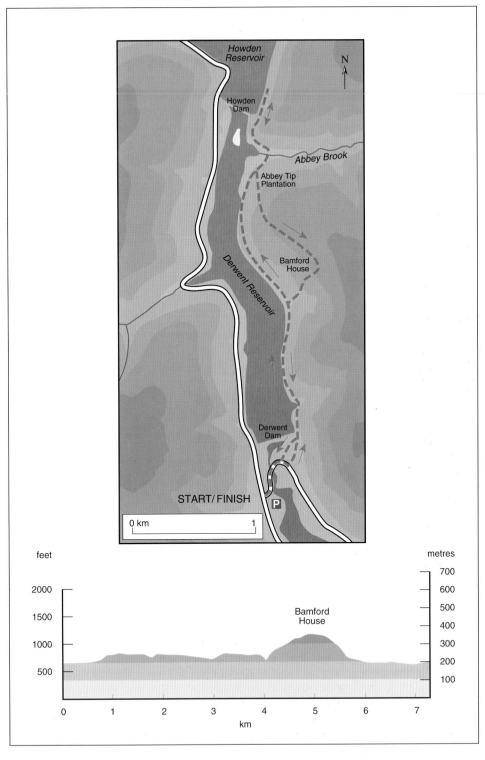

turning to the L to access a narrow path leading further N, which will bring you to the level of Derwent Reservoir. This path, the higher of two, threads its way beneath pine trees, rising on a diagonal towards the top of the dam. Further up, the way passes between rhododendron bushes, and a short distance after this you will reach the dam and Derwent Reservoir.

Cross over an s-stile and veer L to continue N along the broad, gravel-surfaced service track which runs above the E bank of the huge reservoir. Magnificent views now open up on your L across the water towards the low, conifer-covered hillsides on the far side. These are seen at their best on cold and bright autumn days, with the sun illuminating the warm russet colours to absolute perfection beneath a deep blue, cloudless sky. Cross a stone bridge over a feeder stream and continue N along the obvious, perfectly flat way, from which you can concentrate on admiring the splendid views.

Further on, disregard the path leading up to the R, signed to 'Bradfield: Strines'. However, make a mental note of it, as you will be coming back down that way. Continue along the E side of Derwent Reservoir, following its meandering banks which start to converge, reducing the surface area of the water. The wide track then bends gradually to the R, and along here the twin, towered dam which holds back the waters of the higher Howden Reservoir will first come into view. You will then reach Abbey Tip Plantation and a footpath signed 'Ewden via Broomhead: for Bradford and Strines sharp right 40yd ahead'. For now, disregard the higher option and continue along the wide, flat track below. However, you will use this turning on your way back, so again take note.

Your continuation way winds through trees, bending L to cross over Abbey Brook, which tumbles down from the higher terrain of Howden Moors to the E. Pass through the wooden gate on the far side to continue NW, veering N as the track bends around to the R and rises towards Howden Dam above. Ignore a track leading more steeply uphill to your R but branch R further on, selecting the higher of two alternative ways to cover the remaining ground quickly and reach the top of the dam wall. Venture a short distance further N along the banks of Howden Reservoir to obtain unobstructed views of this and the towered dam through gaps in the foliage of the intervening trees, before turning around to commence the walk back to Fairholmes.

Retrace your outward steps to the turning near Abbey Tip which you earlier ignored at MR 171919½. This time, turn off L here and, after less than the stipulated '40yd', turn R along a narrower and rougher side path that winds more steeply up the wooded hillside. Surfaced with stones, this path leads S up a diagonal traverse. Walk through a gap in a dry stone wall and continue uphill along the established diagonal, keeping to the narrow path above the shallow, grassy rut on your L. You will gain height quickly, and if you turn around (and the weather is kind) you will be rewarded by the most magnificent view N along Howden Reservoir.

Cross over a faintly defined grassy path and the traverse will then lead past a sign reading 'Abbey Grange: Strines' (Abbey Grange is where you have just come up from). Here, disregard the grassy way down to your R, which actually peters out, and accept slightly more uphill work by keeping to the way signed to Strines. This continues SE, leading you out into open moorland and across a grassy cart track. The upward gradient then lessens and you will soon find yourself walking along a fairly level path which winds around the hillsides, still heading SE as Derwent Dam comes back into view. Further on, veer R to continue walking close to the dilapidated stone walling to avoid going any further uphill. Just above the ruins of Bamford House, at MR 175912½, fork L along the better-defined path, which then rises gently.

Autumn tints at Derwent Reservoir.

Howden Dam, separating Derwent and Howden Reservoirs.

Ahead, turn full R at the intersection of paths to descend along the one signed 'Public footpath to Derwent Reservoir'. A steepish, sometimes slippery, and rough path leads sw towards Derwent Reservoir below. Lower down, you will be made aware of the re-routing of the path by such notices as 'Erosion control: please keep to path', as an obvious signed way leads to the forested area below, passing through bracken-covered slopes to get there. A steeper zigzag route has to be negotiated along a diverted section, as the rough path enters and threads through the conifers. A final, easy traverse deposits you back on the wide track alongside the reservoir below.

Turn L to walk back, fairly effortlessly, towards Derwent Dam and Fairholmes. Just after reaching the top of the dam, an alternative to following the outward route is to turn R down the stone steps, where you will obtain a really close-up impression of the massive scale of the dam itself, towering ever higher above you to the R as you descend. Walk diagonally left across the grassy area at the bottom, to reconnect with the service road that leads back towards the carpark.

TACKLING THE WALK

CASUAL WALKERS

An ideal half-day walk which should appeal to less energetic walkers, with plenty of interest throughout and just one climb up and down.

FAMILY WALKERS

This route is also suitable for family groups. Those with very small children may prefer to keep to the straight and flat, and spend some time picnicking around the indent at Abbey Tip, where there are some delightful sheltered spots.

STRONG, EXPERIENCED WALKERS

It takes some effort to reach the remote starting point for this walk, and having done so, many strong walkers will wish to extend this short walk by climbing on to the Derwent Edges above, to visit Back Tor and rock formations such as the Cakes of Bread and Salt Cellar.

PLACES OF INTEREST

THE UPPER DERWENT VALLEY

There is an extensive network of footpaths serving the Upper Derwent Valley, centred on Fairholmes. The valley has been flooded by the Howden and Derwent Reservoirs, and in 1943 these waters were used for practice by the famous 617 Dambuster Squadron Lancaster bombers, due to the valley's similarity with the chosen target of the Ruhr Valley dams.

FAIRHOLMES VISITOR CENTRE

Set among sweet-smelling pine trees, this attractive centre provides a range of amenities and has received several accolades. Developed by Severn Trent Water, the site deservedly won the prestigious Conservation Award from the Institute of Chartered Surveyors and *The Times*, together with the Centres of Excellence Award 1993 from the English Forestry Authority.

2 HAYFIELD AND KINDER RESERVOIR

STARTING/ FINISHING POINT
Carpark at Hayfield Visitor Centre OLM 1: MR 036869

GRADING OF WALK
Moderate/ challenging

TIME ALLOWANCE
3½ hours

DISTANCE
7.4km (4.6 miles)

TOTAL HEIGHT GAINED
210m (690ft)

HIGHEST POINT
White Brow (above Kinder Reservoir) 350m (1150ft)

GRADIENTS

Gradual ascent from Hayfield to the N tip of Kinder Reservoir, followed by a steep climb over rough ground to reach Nab Brow. Moderate descent back into Hayfield.

PARKING

Extensive, well laid-out carpark.

PUBLIC TRANSPORT

Bus routes 355, 358, 361, 403, 901 and 902.

OVERVIEW/INTEREST

Starts from the charming village of Hayfield. Woodland section beside the River Kinder with plenty of bird life. Gives a taste of the high, rugged peat moorlands above Kinder Reservoir. Magnificent views along William Clough and of the W edges of Kinder Scout and the Downfall.

AMENITIES

Delightful picnic area, information centre and toilets at the Visitor Centre. More toilets and Ranger Service at the campsite *en route*. Excellent range of hotels, inns, restaurants, cafés and shops catering for walkers in Hayfield.

FOOTPATHS AND WAYSIGNS

Paths are mainly fair to good, but there is some rough ground when climbing up from Kinder Reservoir and in one or two other areas. Very little boggy ground not spanned by adequate bridging. Route is obvious along established paths and few waysigns are needed.

FROM the carpark entrance, cross over Station Road and then use the subway opposite to pass beneath the busy A624 road to enter the centre of Hayfield village. Exit the subway up the ramp on the L, turn R along Walk Mile Road and walk around St Matthew's Parish Church, turning L to complete this. Cross the bridge over the River Sett and turn R along Bank Street, passing by Hayfield Books on your L as you continue uphill. Proceed along

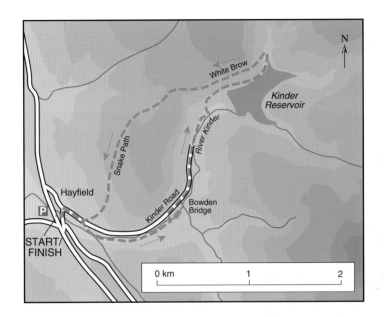

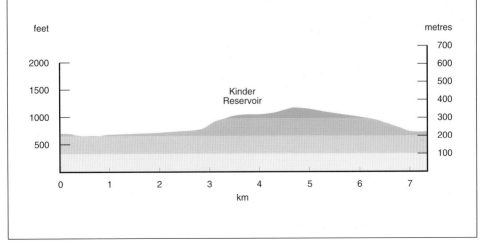

Kinder Road until this bends fairly sharply to the L and at this point continue straight ahead, then walking downhill along Spring Vale Road. Re-cross the river by means of a wooden footbridge and after this turn L when you reach the road ahead. You are now walking E away from Hayfield, following the course of the River Kinder upstream.

A narrowing lane leads beneath trees further up the valley; keep walking along this lane, avoiding several side paths off to the L which cross the stream. When the lane divides ahead, branch L to follow the way nearest to the river, again disregarding further side paths leading off L over it. The track leads to horse stables and just past these you should branch L again to access the public footpath signed 'Kinder via reservoir'. The route next skirts a large but secluded campsite, beyond which the first clear views of the vast, ranging hillsides rising towards mighty Kinder Scout appear. In favourable weather some of the detail of the fascinating rock formations lining the gritstone edges of Kinder plateau are revealed to the E. Keep walking towards these formidable hills, avoiding the side paths off to Kinder Road and Highgate Head which cross your way at right angles.

Pass by the reception centre of the campsite, where a Peak National Park Ranger Service is located, and leave the site over a w-stile adjacent to gates. Public toilets are positioned near this exit. Cross the adjacent lane on a diagonal to your L, cross the river for a third time and then turn R along the surfaced lane signed to 'Kinder Scout via William Clough or Farlands', immediately passing Bowden Bridge carpark with its surrounding high cliff faces (a

A family explore the upper reaches of Kinder Reservoir.

former quarry). Walk past Bowden Bridge Cottage (the name is carved on a former millstone) and continue NE along Kinder Road, walking up gently rising ground. The lane continues up the valley, to bring you to the imposing entrance gates of the driveway to North West Water Kinder Reservoir Treatment Works.

Follow the road around to the R, once again crossing over water by means of a bridge, and then within a further 100 paces turn off L along the waysigned public footpath, which is accessed through a swing gate. The way continues along a leafy, shaded embankment beside the River Kinder and it does become muddy in places after prolonged rain. The ground rises at the far end of the embankment and you will cross a metal bridge on your L to reach (on the far side of the drive of the water treatment plant) the continuation route leading to 'Open Country'. This is waysigned with a blue arrowhead as a public bridleway.

Through another swing gate, the continuation route leads quite steeply upwards along an enclosed, cobble-surfaced way. As you climb, spectacular new vistas will appear ahead to your R. These take in the impressive, grassy dam wall holding back the catchment waters of Kinder Reservoir and, high above, the eroded, crumbling rocky edges which form the W rim of Kinder Scout to the ENE. The steepish incline will level off just before you reach the NW tip of the reservoir at the dam. Here another path converges on your L from above, and at this junction turn to your R to identify the twin peaks of Mount Famine and South Head rising majestically as pointed, grassy knolls to the S.

Continue walking between E and NE above the reservoir, starting this section by negotiating some shallow steps. The path undulates down and then up more steps, progressively gaining further marginal height. Cross a small feeder stream and beyond this go through a swing gate to enter an environmentally sensitive area of moorland. Access to this remains open and a footpath sign indicates the line of the continuation path, which traverses around the hillside through dense bracken.

Towards the NE end of the reservoir the path swings around to the L heading towards the indent of William Clough which rises ahead to the N. Go through another swing gate and a short distance further on you will reach an intersection of paths. These converge close to a wooden bridge spanning the stream on your R, at MR 059887. Ahead the way leads up William Clough, while across the footbridge a challenging climb leads to the edge of Kinder Scout. Neither of these paths is for you: instead, your continuation path ascends less formidable hillsides, beginning by backtracking acutely to your L and following the rough, narrow path which traverses the higher ground to the SW. This leads you up steepish slopes covered with a mixture of bilberry and bracken.

*Looking across
Kinder Reservoir
towards the
western edges
of Kinder Scout.*

Near the top of the slope the path degenerates into an eroded funnel and this demands care. Beyond this, the route connects with a wider, better-defined path (Snake Path), along which you turn L to commence your circuitous, higher-level return towards Hayfield. A fairly level stretch follows, allowing you to concentrate on the superb views to the S of vast, open landscapes stretching away towards Kinder Scout and South Head beyond the tranquil waters of the reservoir.

However, be careful when the paths divide to branch R along the narrower, higher way. This continuation path then traverses around a heather-covered hillside, seen to perfection in late August when the ground is turned deep purple by the heather flowers. You will gradually gain further height, and some distance further on the path will bend around to the R to lead you across flatter, high moorland terrain, which is the habitat of the grouse (and on occasions the grouse shooter – note the shooting cabin on the OLM).

Pass by the bridleway leading off to your L and then bear L along the wide, level gravel path signed 'Hayfield 1½ miles'. Along here expansive moorlands occupy the ground on your R, which rises to the pointed peak of The Knott to the NNW. Signs of habitation surrounding Hayfield soon come into view directly ahead and the continuation path snakes towards these along the appropriately named path. You will reach a wooden gate at the boundary of 'Open Country', which you are now about to leave. Avoid a side path leading off to the R in the direction of Cown Edge, the long flat ridge far away to the NW.

Go through the wrought-iron K-gate, one of several to come, and continue walking SW on the wide, sandy path, disregarding a cart track by forking L and then traversing around a grassy hillside ahead. The obvious way continues beside a section of stone wall on your R, and it then leads through a second iron K-gate before bearing further L downhill towards the buildings of Hayfield. The continuing descent leads you to, along and then through (by means of a choice of gates) another section of dry stone walling. A diagonal to your R then passes above a small cluster of mature beech trees to reach yet another iron K-gate. Beyond this, your established downward diagonal uses a section of rougher path to connect with an S-stile positioned at a metal gate. A final K-gate is then negotiated before the path bends sharply to the L, to bring you to the buildings of Hayfield below.

At the bottom of the path, turn R along Kinder Road to continue your descent into the centre of Hayfield. A short distance along this road you will connect with your outward route, and from this point you simply retrace your earlier steps back to the carpark on the far side of the main A624 road.

TACKLING THE WALK

CASUAL WALKERS

This route is very suitable for most walkers, providing a taste of wilder terrain and superb views, and penetrating open moorlands along safe, well-used paths.

FAMILY WALKERS

The walk can also be enjoyed by families with older children. It is probably too difficult for tiny tots, and such family groups are advised to turn back when they reach the reservoir and perhaps spend more time exploring the lower ground between there and Hayfield.

STRONG, EXPERIENCED WALKERS

This is an enjoyable short, circular walk in its own right, but dedicated walkers may wish to combine it with a longer, more challenging route on to Kinder Scout, using either William Clough or the ridge leading up to Sandy Heys to reach the plateau.

PLACES OF INTEREST

HAYFIELD

Hayfield is an attractive village, well served by public transport and considered to be one of the principal w gateways to the Dark Peak. Nowadays it caters mainly for visitors, tourists and walkers, although sheep farming is still important in the surrounding hills. Previously, its economy was industrial, related in sequence to wool, cotton, calico printing and paper making.

KINDER RESERVOIR

Water conservation remains a feature of the district and the irregularly shaped Kinder Reservoir lies about 2km (1¼m) to the NE of Hayfield. Although access is unfortunately restricted, the reservoir occupies a fine setting and is a welcome and almost indispensable landmark for walkers venturing E-W across the high ground of Kinder Scout, especially in clinging, misty weather.

3 EDALE, GRINDSBROOK AND GRINDSLOW KNOLL

**STARTING/
FINISHING POINT**
Carpark below Edale
Village OLM 1: MR
124853

**GRADING
OF WALK**
Moderate/
challenging

**TIME
ALLOWANCE**
4 hours

DISTANCE
6.9km (4.3 miles)

**TOTAL HEIGHT
GAINED**
420m (1380ft)

HIGHEST POINT
Grindslow Knoll
601m (1970ft)

GRADIENTS
Long, relatively hard climb from Edale to the top of Kinder Edges, and another ascent to reach Grindslow Knoll, the highest point of the walk. Steep descent back into Edale.

PARKING
Large, well-appointed but expensive coach and carpark. Alternative, cheaper parking beyond the nearby Edale Cottage Café.

PUBLIC TRANSPORT
Bus routes 260 and 403. Train service linking Manchester and Sheffield.

OVERVIEW/INTEREST
Starts from the attractive village of Edale, official start of the Pennine Way. Route passes through wild and remote gritstone landscapes. Includes a scramble up a rockfall to reach the edge of Kinder Scout. Magnificent, challenging scenery all around. Interesting, weathered rock features and formations.

AMENITIES
Toilets at the carpark. Refreshment facilities (inns and cafés) in Edale village. Combined Peak National Park Visitor Centre, Ranger Service and Rescue Post at Fieldhead near the church, which also offer refreshments.

FOOTPATHS AND WAYSIGNS
Paths vary from wide routes refurbished with large flagstones to narrow, rough channels across boggy ground and exposed bedrock. Minor scrambling required up a rockfall in the upper reaches of Grindsbrook Clough. Some erosion in places along sections of the well-trodden route. Very few waysigns away from Edale, but route is always fairly obvious.

L EAVE the carpark by going down the steps next to the toilet block and turn R to walk through the elongated village of Edale, passing almost immediately beneath the railway line at Edale Station. (The Edale Cottage Café is to the L just before the railway bridge.) The side lane through the village leads past the Rambler

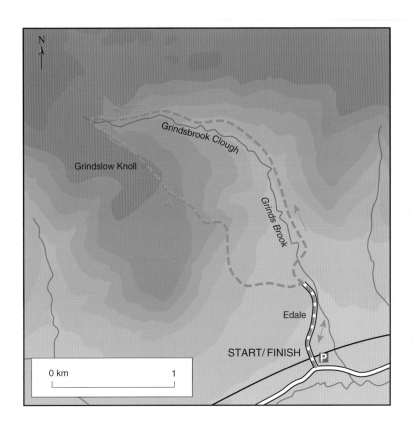

N

Grindsbrook Clough

Grindslow Knoll

Grinds Brook

Edale

START/ FINISH

P

0 km   1

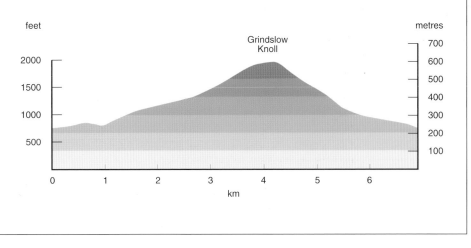

feet   metres

Grindslow
Knoll

                                                                                    700
2000   600
                                                                                    500
1500   400
1000   300
                                                                                    200
500   100

0   1   2   3   4   5   6

km

The gritty north-western panorama from Grindslow Knoll.

Inn, the Peak National Park Visitor Centre and the spired church of the Holy and Undivided Trinity, to reach the Old Nag's Head Inn (built in 1577) towards the top end of the village. The massive slopes leading to Kinder Scout rise majestically ahead, this gigantic plateau effectively blocking off any more distant views to the N. To your rear the unstable slopes of Mam Tor, the 'shivering mountain' (see page 40), do likewise to the s. Further on, more of the undulating ridge from Mam Tor to Lose Hill is revealed to the E, including the steep, eroded, crumbling cliff face of Back Tor to the ESE, partway along this mighty spur.

Continue up the lane next to the inn, heading further N up the valley, and beyond the cottages bear L along the waysigned footpath. However, within a further 100 paces you should turn off R down a narrow public footpath signed to 'Grindsbrook'. Descend a flight of stone steps and then cross over Grinds Brook (the stream) via a railed footbridge positioned beneath trees. More steps lead up from the narrow clough, and partway up these you will pass through a swing gate. (Near this point is an area of sapling trees planted by the pupils of Edale Primary School in 1990, during National Tree Week.) An obvious, flagstoned (refurbished) way then leads around to the L further along the clough and into more open countryside.

Further on, disregard the footpath zigzagging steeply up on your R, which leads towards the rocky tor of Ringing Roger located on the rim of Kinder Scout. The clear continuation way threads through redundant stone gateposts, and as you approach these more superb views open up on your L, above the trees, of the steep, grassy slopes rising towards Grindslow Knoll – your principal objective – to the NW. Your path leads towards a copse of mixed trees ahead; in good weather, just before entering these you should turn around to take in the superb view back down the valley towards Edale, with the undulating ridge of Rushup Edge, Mam Tor and Lose Hill framing the distant horizon to the S.

Be warned: the entrance to the narrow strip of woodland is through a powerful spring-loaded gate, as is the exit a short distance further on. This second gate and the associated dry stone wall mark the boundary of 'Open Country', and from this point you will be able to position the craggy peak of Ringing Roger, rising on your R to the NE. Cross the tributary watercourse by the footbridge to enter the wilder and more remote middle reaches of Grindsbrook Clough, thereby avoiding the narrow path leading uphill towards Ringing Roger on your R. From here, the valley progressively narrows and steepens, and the path simultaneously becomes rougher. However, the well-used and eroded continuation way presents few problems as it winds above the meandering stream, tracking its course up the clough.

You will cross another tributary watercourse at an acute bend ahead, where the highest-positioned trees lining the clough – a group of tattered, windswept silver birch – will be left behind. The route continues to gain further height to the NW, where the steepening slopes are covered with an attractive pattern of intermingled heather and bilberry. Several miniature waterfalls in the fast-flowing brook below add further interest to this remote scene. The steepening path eventually reaches a badly eroded, crumbling face which you should track around to the L using a narrow, eroded path in order to reach the level of the stream. Then clamber up the fixed rocks and loose boulders flanking the R bank of the stream, until more difficult ground looms up ahead. Here there is a fairly obvious, natural crossing point which you should use to reach the L bank of the brook, where you must locate and follow a faint track leading further upstream. (Note that there are alternative ways up this section of the route.)

The more spectacular upper reaches of Grindsbrook Clough now beckon you. These are two fangs of rockfalls which line the steep and narrow dividing clefts. Either of these will lead you to the edge of Kinder Scout. Continue up the L one, which will take you to the edge of Kinder nearer to Grindslow Knoll. The ascent now crosses rough, boulder-strewn ground and on occasion you will need to use your hands to steady yourself as you progress upwards. Pause for breath partway up in order to spot the distinctively shaped Anvil Stone perched above you to the W (you will shortly walk past this landmark). The immediate surroundings now become increasingly spectacular, with an assortment of irregular gritstone edges, tumbled-down boulders, rock faces and a gushing stream enfolding you in a breathtaking enclosed setting. However, you will soon be standing on the edge of Kinder, from where you will be able to gaze down on wider landscapes spreading outwards for miles below you. You have already positioned the major geographical features, but directly ahead to the N there are glimpses of the boulder-strewn, acid moorlands which form the considerable bulk of Kinder Scout – a formidable landscape of peat hags which stretch away as far as the eye can see.

From your final direction of approach to the edge, turn sharp L to continue walking SE along the indented edge of Kinder, tracking towards the rounded shape of Grindslow Knoll and almost immediately passing the weathered shape of the Anvil Stone, balanced precariously to your L. The fairly obvious, sandy continuation path then snakes high above the void of Grindsbrook to lead you directly towards the higher slopes of Grindslow Knoll, about 0.5km (¼ mile) further on. Aim your final approach directly for the sprawling summit cairn, avoiding the path traversing around to the L of the pointed peak. On a fine day, the all-round panorama from this lofty viewing platform is stunning. From a height of 601m (1970ft) much of the Vale of Edale is revealed, as is the complete length of the long, undulating spur extending from Lose Hill in the E to Rushup Edge in the W. The vast hinterland of the Kinder wilderness rises to the N with the high spot of the somewhat paradoxically named Kinder Low rising as an apparently tiny blip above the expansive, flattish landscapes to the W. Beyond these features, hills regress in all directions, even to the N beyond the far-away Kinder skyline.

Start your descent by locating and following the eroded, sandy way which tracks SE in the direction of Edale village. The initial section is steep and the descent here can become tricky when the ground is frozen and covered with ice or snow, so take extra care in these conditions. Further down, the continuation path becomes progressively less demanding and your speed will increase. The clear, wide way follows the contours of the hillsides as it snakes down, keeping to a SE diagonal as it leads you closer to Edale. The rough but well-used route then bends to the R, bringing you to an s-stile and gate combination at the boundary of 'Open Country'. Continue on your established descent line, soon following a much more agreeable, grassy track.

The route then descends through a wide gap in a wooden fence, next to which is an apparently redundant stile! A short distance beyond this your descent path connects with a variant of the famous Pennine Way. Here, instead of using the s-stile on your R, veer L to complete the remaining short distance into the village of

Edale. The way leads through another spring-loaded gate and then runs alongside a tree-fringed brook to reach the official starting point of the Pennine Way walk to Kirk Yetholm – some 440km (275 miles) away! Go through a K-gate, turn R, and then retrace your earlier steps down through the village and past the church back to the carpark below.

TACKLING THE WALK

CASUAL WALKERS
This is a challenging but very rewarding route, well within the capabilities of most reasonably fit walkers. It will provide casual walkers with a taste of wild, fairly difficult terrain and could stimulate the appetite for more of the same. On the way up, if you feel the challenges ahead are too much, just turn around.

FAMILY WALKERS
Older children will enjoy this energetic climb and stimulating descent, but the complete route will almost certainly be beyond the capabilities and enjoyment of younger ones. Those with tiny tots are advised to walk partway up Grindsbrook, find a safe, sheltered playspot beside the brook and watch the more energetic pass by.

STRONG, EXPERIENCED WALKERS
This is an exhilarating, short half-day outing for strong and proficient walkers. Having reached the edge of Kinder, however, many will wish to extend the route by tracking further along the edges of the plateau. Two circuits ideal for this purpose are either W to Kinder Low, Edale Cross and then down Jacob's Ladder, or E, taking in Ringing Roger and perhaps even venturing as far as Jaggers Clough.

PLACES OF INTEREST

EDALE
The delightful, elongated village of Edale hugs a wooded dell carved by the lower reaches of Grinds Brook. It originally served the surrounding sheep-farming community but nowadays is a busy tourist centre catering for walkers and other visitors. As well as the amenities detailed on page 30, it has a fine spired church – the Holy and Undivided Trinity – and several comfortable guest houses providing bed and breakfast. However, its main claim to fame among the walking fraternity is that it remains the official starting point for the Pennine Way, the forerunner of all long-distance walking routes in this country.

4 MAM TOR AND HOLLINS CROSS (CAVERNS AND MINES)

**STARTING/
FINISHING POINT**
Car park below Mam
Nick OLM 1: MR
123832

**GRADING
OF WALK**
Moderate/
challenging

**TIME
ALLOWANCE**
3 hours

DISTANCE
5.8km (3.6 miles)

**TOTAL HEIGHT
GAINED**
270m (875ft)

HIGHEST POINT
Mam Tor 517m
(1695ft)

GRADIENTS
Short, sharp climb at the start, followed by a walk along an undulating ridge. More gradual descent, with other minor ups and downs.

PARKING
Secluded, tiered carpark, adjacent to the A625 road, holds over 50 vehicles but fills up quickly.

PUBLIC TRANSPORT
Bus routes 260 and 403.

OVERVIEW/INTEREST
Magnificent views from the top of Mam Tor. Superb ridge walk follows to Hollins Cross. Opportunity to see the devastation caused to the A625 road by the unstable 'shivering mountain' high above. Route passes by Treak Cliff Cavern and Blue John Cavern and Mine.

AMENITIES
No facilities at the carpark but Castleton and Edale are only short car journeys away. Refreshments *en route* at Treak Cliff Cavern.

FOOTPATHS AND WAYSIGNS
Paths variable to excellent, with few waterlogged areas. Some erosion still has to be dealt with. Signs adequate where most needed.

FROM the top level of the carparking area, walk N up the exit steps. The continuation path at the top of these bends to the R to traverse further up the grassy slopes which lead to the summit of Mam Tor. When you emerge from the screening trees you will be welcomed by the sight of vast landscapes down on your R, consisting of open pastures interspersed with folded hillsides and the chasm of the Winnats Pass snaking away to the SE. The path then connects with the road threading through Mam Nick and down into the Vale of Edale, and also with another footpath coming up on your R. Climb over one of the combination stiles to enter

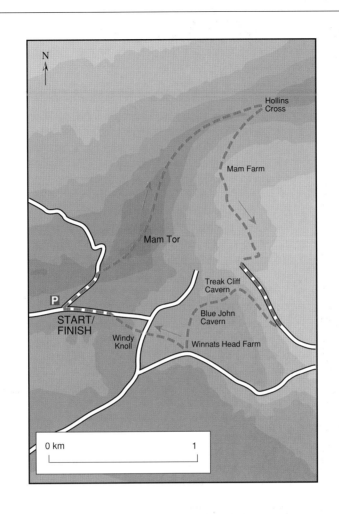

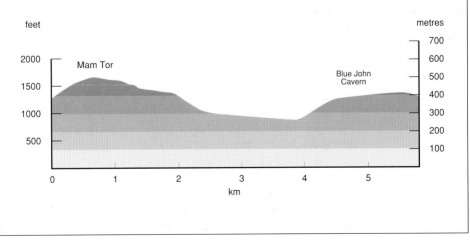

37

the High Peak Estate of Mam Tor and continue climbing along the obvious stepway of railed pavement stones. This permanently refurbished way leads NE directly to the summit of Mam Tor, the highest point of the walk.

Mam Tor commands a height of 517m (1695ft) and in clear weather the panorama from its summit is breathtaking. Start by looking N across the sheltered lowland pastures of the Vale of Edale to the long, serrated edges of mighty Kinder Scout, which stretch for several kilometres at a height of around 600m (2000ft). At the w end of the valley the path up Jacob's Ladder presents an entrance to – or escape from – the valley, depending on your direction of travel, while further E the attractive village of Edale straddles the tree-lined gully cut by Grinds Brook.

Also competing for your attention is the majestic, undulating ridge upon which you are standing: this extends E to its grassy terminus at Lose Hill and w along Rushup Edge. Vast tracts of open countryside stretch away to the S, rising to the distant landscapes of Old Moor, and from these uplands Cave Dale and the Winnats link this higher ground with the flat, sheltered Hope Valley, with its orderly pastures and attractive villages of Castleton and Hope. The whole is a quite superb cocktail of the shales, grits and sandstones of the Dark Peak, blended with the carboniferous limestones of the White Peak.

From the trig point, descend along the narrowing ridge, initially tracking NE and then E as the path bends to the R, more directly in line with Back Tor and Lose Hill. You will lose height as you proceed, crossing over two stiles as you make your way along the apex of the spur down to Hollins Cross. This is a wide, shallow hause and the meeting place of several paths. The spot is identified by a memorial stone pillar dedicated to the memory of Tom Hyett of Long Eaton and erected by a group from the Ramblers' Association in 1964. From here, your descent continues down a narrow path to the R, but be careful in selecting this as two paths lead down this flank of the spur into the Hope Valley: yours is the one sharp R, which tracks SW along a diagonal directly towards Mam Tor. This rougher path traverses quite steeply down the grassy slopes, and lower down the well-trodden way leads over a stile positioned within gorse thickets.

The path often becomes muddy around here as a consequence of competing with the course of a drainage stream flowing down the hillside. You will cross two more stiles in quick succession, at the same time ignoring a narrow path leading off uphill to the R. The path then threads through clumps of gorse and a plantation of trees containing beech, birch and Scots pine. Then, just above Mam Farm, you will reach another junction of ways, nestling within a group of more mature trees including birch, oak and rowan. Your waymarked path skirts above the attractively positioned farm buildings to cross another stile, before dropping down quite steeply over a grassy brow to reach the entrance track to the farm at MR 133841.

The farm track is accessed by another stile, near to which is an information plaque describing the woodland conservation area through which you have just descended. Now turn R along the wide, fenced track and follow its bends further downhill. When you reach more stone outbuildings, turn sharp L and then use the P-stile ahead – adjacent to the gable end of the buildings – to enter the meadowlands below. Continue your descent across these fields, now walking s directly in line with the pointed peak of Treak Cliff, some distance away. The grassy way leads to a stile straddling a wire fence, above and to the R of a wooden gate. Veer L to regain the more distinct, narrow path and keep to this as it continues to undulate downhill. Further on the path divides, and yours is the narrower one of compacted earth, to the R and nearer to the fence.

The continuation path winds down towards a clump of trees, passing an interesting small, reeded bog pool which justifies the slight diversion. Past this, the side path reconnects with the wider, grassy way down, and from here you follow the merged routes to

The start of the descent from Hollins Cross.

reach and cross two more stiles breaching wire fencing. Then bear R to reach the connection with a path coming up from Castleton. Turn sharp R at this junction to proceed around a small plantation of Scots pine and willow, following the path as it bends to the L. You will then cross a tiny brook and enter an area of disused mine workings, which still contain interesting remnants from the days of sweat and toil. Beyond these remains, you will reach the road at a wooden gate.

Your continuation route is L down the road, but before you do this make another slight detour to inspect the remains of Odin Mine, some 100 paces away uphill to the R, next to the bus turning area. After this, walk downhill for about 0.5km (¼ mile) to reach Treak Cliff Cavern, above to your R. Climb up the long flight of concrete steps to reach the entrance; partway up you must ignore the path off to the L, prominently signed to the 'Winnats', to arrive at the refreshment/gift shop at the cavern, well worth a visit. Afterwards, climb up more steps and then turn R to follow the signed public footpath which leads above the buildings. Clamber over the stile ahead to enter open countryside once again.

From here, a narrow path of compacted earth traverses uphill across grassy slopes, revealing further fine views – of which the one towards Back Tor and Lose Hill to the NE is supreme. You will gain further height as you walk towards the gouged-out, concave slopes of Mam Tor, the 'shivering mountain', where the successive layering of softer shales and harder gritstones which cause its instability are revealed. Higher up, the path becomes rougher as it bends around to the L to track above a narrow, grassy gully on your R. You will reach a choice of stiles, where your continuation way is over the L one and past the nearby waysigned post (yellow arrowhead). From here, a wide, grassy way leads W over the brow ahead to bring you to the Blue John Cavern and Mine (there is a shop at the entrance), reached beyond an L-stile.

Leave over the stile positioned at the far end of the mine buildings and follow the waysigned footpath further uphill. The way then bends L towards Winnats Head Farm. At the boundary walling of the farm, turn R to continue along the footpath signed to 'Mam Tor'. Climb over the stile and cross the adjacent field and then the minor road ahead, using the stiles to negotiate the stone retaining walls on either side of the roadway. Cross the exposed – and appropriately named – grassy slopes of Windy Knoll, veering R when the path divides. From here, head directly towards the tree-enclosed parking area below Mam Nick. In getting there, your path connects with another path descending from the direction of Old Moor, and you should turn R along the better-defined way to reach the A525 road. Turn L along the road and the carpark is a short distance further on.

TACKLING THE WALK

CASUAL WALKERS

This walk is suitable for most casual walkers: it is not too demand-ing, but some effort is needed to complete the route. The rewards are superb scenery, interesting caverns and mines to visit, and a real sense of achievement to be savoured at the end.

FAMILY WALKERS

Similar remarks apply here as for casual walkers. Tiny tots, unless being carried, will almost certainly find the complete route much too strenuous. You could take them all or part of the way up to the summit of Mam Tor, return to your vehicle, and then visit either or both of the caverns.

STRONG, EXPERIENCED WALKERS

This is an interesting short walk, suitable for an evening ramble. However, many strong walkers will wish to complete the whole of the ridge to and beyond Lose Hill, and there are a number of dif-ferent ways of returning from this end point to Mam Nick.

PLACES OF INTEREST

TREAK CLIFF CAVERN

Described as an underground wonderland, Treak Cliff Cavern, Castleton, contains stalactites, stalagmites, flowstone rock, Blue John stone and a great variety of minerals and fossils, all in a series of caves with such intriguing names as the Dream Cave, Aladdin's Cave, the Fairyland Grotto, the Dome of St Paul's, the Fossil Cave and the Witches' Cave. On display you will also see the largest piece of Blue John ever found: it weighs around 16 tonnes.

BLUE JOHN CAVERN AND MINE

This cave complex is also located near to Castleton, opposite Mam Tor. Again, there are a series of interconnected caverns with such captivating names as the Grand Crystallized Cavern, the Waterfall Cavern, the Stalactite Cavern, Lord Mulgrave's Dining Room and the Variegated Cavern. These display an assortment of features among which are fossils, including the Sea Lily and corals, Blue John stone, and those such as stalactites and stalagmites formed by water permeating through carboniferous limestone over millions of years.

5 HOPE AND WIN HILL

**STARTING/
FINISHING POINT**
Carpark in Hope
village centre
OLM 1: MR 171835

**GRADING
OF WALK**
Moderate/
challenging

**TIME
ALLOWANCE**
4 hours

DISTANCE
9.3km (5.8 miles)

**TOTAL HEIGHT
GAINED**
300m (985ft)

HIGHEST POINT
Win Hill 462m
(1515ft)

GRADIENTS

Steady climb to the top of Win Hill, with some fairly steep sections.
Reverse of this on the way down.

PARKING

Carpark holds about 25 cars, with space for four coaches.

PUBLIC TRANSPORT

Bus routes 173, 174, 181, 197, 202, 254, 274, 276, 280, 309, 395, 400 and
403. Train service, Manchester to Sheffield line.

OVERVIEW/INTEREST

Walk of great variety, from sheltered woodlands and lowland pastures
to exposed ridges and tors. Splendid views over Ladybower
Reservoir towards Derwent Edges. Plenty of wildlife, including
badgers.

AMENITIES

Toilets at the carpark. Selection of inns, cafés and shops in Hope village.
No convenient refreshment *en route*.

FOOTPATHS AND WAYSIGNS

Paths are mostly good, well-drained and secure. Some erosion in places
and the odd muddy patch after heavy rain. Signs a mixture, generally
there when needed but some omissions!

FROM the carpark entrance, cross the busy A625 road diagonally
to your R and walk past Hope Garage and the Woodbine Café
opposite. Turn L at Blacksmith's Cottage along the way signed
'Public footpath Losehill Farm 1', departing N from the village. Pass
through the iron K-gate and fine views will immediately open up
on your L of Mam Tor to the W and Lose Hill to the NW. Continue
through a second K-gate and then along the avenue ahead (Eccles
Close), where you will pass Hope Clinic on your R. Cross over the
road directly opposite and then squeeze through the narrow

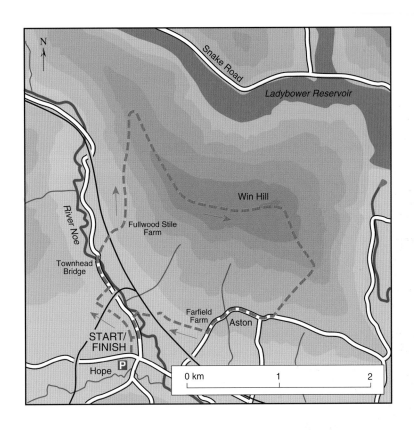

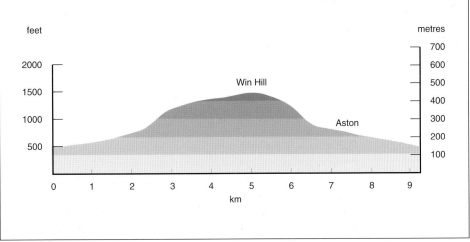

G-stile to the L of Hope County Primary School to access the continuation footpath.

A grassy way now leads slightly uphill beside a hawthorn hedge on your R. Ahead, the waymarked route leading towards Lose Hill passes through two more G-stiles before resuming its progress uphill, now adjacent to a more mature hawthorn hedge. Track L to negotiate two S-stiles and then keep to the line of a fence, walking past a redundant stile to reach the railway line further on. The broad shoulder of Win Hill now appears to your R towards the NE, with the pointed tip of its summit – your main objective – just visible above the intervening slopes. Cross the railway line by means of the concrete footbridge, negotiating the stiles at either end as you go. Walk across the grassy area on the far side and pass through another G-stile to enter a surfaced lane. As directed, follow the signed public footpath around to the L and walk past a bungalow.

Beyond the adjacent yard of the bungalow, be careful to turn R when the footpaths divide ahead, climbing over another stile to continue NE and head more directly towards Win Hill, far above. This leads you down to the road through the Vale of Edale, accessed by means of an unusual S-stile. Turn L along the road: beware of fast-moving traffic, particularly as you get down from the stile. When you reach the vicinity of Underleigh Country House, bear R along the road (ignoring the side lane on your L) and then use Townhead Bridge to cross over the River Noe. Just beyond this, leave the Edale Road by walking NE straight on up the surfaced lane for some distance, in summer enjoying the cooling shade of mature deciduous trees, mainly sycamore.

You will soon reach open country again, and here there are fleeting views through nearby foliage of the summit cone of Lose Hill over to your L. The continuation way crosses over the main railway line at bridge 39 (MR 169848) and this now indicates that more serious climbing lies ahead. When you reach Fullwood Stile Farm a short distance further on the continuation route bends sharply L, tracking further uphill beneath an archway of trees. Continue walking N, ignoring a farm track leading off through a gateway to your R. Be careful here to keep to the main path, identified as a fairly straight, hedged diagonal. Further on beyond a metal gate, veer R along the more open way which continues to rise up steeper, bracken-covered slopes over rougher, rockier ground.

The vast, rounded slopes rising to the massive plateau of Kinder Scout now appear ahead to your L towards the NW with the wide, picturesque Vale of Edale curving away between this massif and the long, undulating ridge linking Mam Tor and Lose Hill. Further on, an alternating grassy and then stony surface winds up and around the brow of the hillside, to pass an isolated stone pillar and

after this lead you to the apex of a broad, grassy ridge, the flank of which you have been scaling for some distance. Ahead there is a vast forestry plantation of Scots pine. Follow the wide, grassy way as it bends to the R to gain the ridge and then turn full R when you reach the intersection of paths ahead. From here, begin walking s towards a dilapidated stone wall and another solitary stone pillar, which you again pass close by.

Looking back towards Hope.

Continue walking SE and then E along the curving ridge as it gains further height, heading towards the rocky tor of Win Hill which, in clear weather, is now visible ahead, also to the SE. In such weather the all-round panorama from this approach is breathtaking, and in addition to the features already positioned, new and spectacular vistas open up on your L to the NE of the vast, high moorland landscapes cupping the Upper Derwent Valley. Keep walking along the ascending apex of the ridge, ignoring all side paths leading off to both L and R. Further on there is a remarkable first sighting of the splendid arched concrete road bridge which spans Ladybower Reservoir majestically, carrying the A57 Snake Road across the water.

Cross over a stile and then, after an intersection of ways at which you keep straight on, you will reach the final steep, rocky slopes forming the craggy summit of Win Hill. There is a choice of ways to the top: the path snakes around to the R before turning L to reach the highest point, while for the more adventurous there is an easy scramble up the rocky spur formed by a jumble of boulders. In clear weather, the cheese-wedge shape of the summit of Win Hill (or Winhill Pike), standing at 462m (1515ft), provides a superb viewing platform for all directions. New landscapes open up to the E towards the succession of gritstone edges circling above Hathersage; the Ladybower, Derwent and Howden Reservoir complex stretches away to the N into the Upper

Ladybower Reservoir and the Derwent Edges, observed from the summit of Win Hill.

Derwent Valley, with the Vale of Edale and the Lose Hill to Mam Tor ridge doing the same to the W.

Descend to the E along the rocky ridge, following the obvious continuation footpath. The initial section of the way down is across rough, stony ground and you will need to be vigilant to maintain your footing. The descent will bring you to a recently

positioned P-stile and steps spanning a dry stone wall. Branch off R just below these to follow a grassy way snaking down at a comfortable gradient across the expansive heather- and bilberry-covered slopes. Your changed direction is first to the S, then veering SE, before returning to S as the path contorts down the hillside. The last time I came this way I had the thrill of seeing a grown badger scurrying for cover across the hillside. On the far side of a dilapidated stone wall be careful to keep straight on, disregarding a grassy way which leads more steeply down to the R.

Your direction of travel has now reverted to SE again along a narrow sheep track. This relatively indistinct section soon connects with a wider, better-defined path along which you turn R to continue walking down a traverse that circles further R around the hillside. In doing this your direction gradually changes towards the W, in line with far-away Mam Tor. The way leads down to an S-stile across a high stone wall which it is essential to use – but be prepared for the unexpectedly steep fall-away on the far side! Cross the field below, initially keeping towards the boundary to the L, close to a hawthorn hedge. Walk to the bottom corner to cross an S-stile breaching a wooden fence. An enclosed way leads further downhill, and after you have passed some stone walling an elevated bank on the L funnels down to a somewhat obscurely sited S-stile. Beyond this, an overgrown enclosed path leads down to the surfaced lane ahead, where there are two drinking troughs.

Turn R and walk gently uphill past Aston Hall and through Aston. Ignore the branch lane on the L and continue downhill along Aston Lane, ignoring another footpath leading off to the L further on. Keep walking along the back lane as it curves downhill to the L after passing Croft Head and Yew Tree Farm, and then spurn yet another path on the L, this one signed to 'Hope Station'. Continue along the lane until you reach Farfield Farm, where you should turn R to pass through an imposing stone gateway with carved pillars. Ahead, bear L to pass below the farm as you walk along a wide, waysigned track. Disregard the path leading off through a K-gate on the L and continue down the wide gravel and stony track. You will pass Hope cemetery and then a short distance further on your descent will connect with a surfaced lane.

Turn L and use the lane to re-cross the River Noe by means of a stone bridge. The lane then leads to the road between Hope and Edale, along which you should turn L again in the direction of Hope. Just past the school, turn R along Eccles Close and then L, to retrace your outward steps back to the carpark in the centre of the village.

TACKLING THE WALK

CASUAL WALKERS

This is a very satisfying outing for less ambitious walkers with a steady climb to start with, a taste of the high moorlands, the thrill of standing on top of a craggy, weathered tor and a final section through sheltered rural countryside.

FAMILY WALKERS

Similar remarks apply to family walkers, especially those with sturdy youngsters. Families with small children could do a shorter circuit, missing out Win Hill and descending from the ridge via Twitchill Farm, but be warned there is one steep, often slippery section on this way down.

STRONG, EXPERIENCED WALKERS

This is a fine short walk in its own right, but it can easily be extended by walking down to Ladybower Reservoir, or made into a really challenging route by looping in Lose Hill and perhaps part of the Mam Tor ridge.

PLACES OF INTEREST

HOPE

The village of Hope has been in existence for over 1000 years, and at one time its parish embraced a large part of the Royal Forest of the High Peak including Buxton, Tideswell and Chapel-en-le-Frith. It has a weekly market, an educational college was opened in 1958 and sheep farming is still important in the surrounding area. Although not as popular with general tourists as its nearby neighbours Castleton and Edale, it is favoured by walkers as a starting point for walks to Win and Lose Hills and also along the Hope Valley to either the Winnats or in the opposite direction towards Hathersage.

WIN HILL

This craggy, weathered tor of sandstone and gritstone rising to 462m (1515ft) is located some 2km (1¼ miles) to the NE of Hope village. The twin peak of Lose Hill, at the E end of the Mam Tor ridge, lies close by and it is said that these two names are related to a nearby battle fought in 626 AD between the kings of Wessex and Northumberland. Edwin of Northumberland was the 'winner' and he happened to occupy 'Win' Hill. It is reported that the River Noe ran red on that ill-fated day.

49

6 HIGGER TOR, BURBAGE ROCKS AND CARL WARK

STARTING/ FINISHING POINT
Roadside verges below Higger Tor
OLM 1: MR 256822

GRADING OF WALK
Easy/straight-forward

TIME ALLOWANCE
2½ hours

DISTANCE
5.8km (3.6 miles)

TOTAL HEIGHT GAINED
185m (605ft)

HIGHEST POINT
Higger Tor 434m (1425ft)

GRADIENTS
Two modest climbs to the top of Higger Tor, the second by way of Carl Wark, which is an up and down *en route*.

PARKING
Safe space for 10–15 cars in laybys and on roadside verges.

PUBLIC TRANSPORT
Bus route 257.

OVERVIEW/INTEREST
Rocks and boulders galore! Features the craggy peak of Higger Tor and Carl Wark Iron Age settlement. Opportunity to see climbers on Burbage Rocks. Route is continuously full of interest, circling through wild and remote, rocky terrain.

AMENITIES
No toilets or refreshment facilities available on this walk. Attractive village of Hathersage nearby offers some splendid hotels and inns.

FOOTPATHS AND WAYSIGNS
Paths are good to excellent for most of the way, with some rougher sections and the possibility of minor scrambling. Virtually no water-logged ground, but there are streams to be forded and significant erosion in places. Very few directional signs are needed or provided.

THE walk commences among wild, remote and spectacular mountain scenery and continues like this the whole way around! Right from the start, the tumble of gritstone edges, rock faces and boulders forming the high ground of Higger Tor is silhouetted above you, a short distance away to the sw. Clear views of this spectacular feature will remain with you for the rest of the way.

Cross the road and climb over the wooden s-stile to access the wide, stepped footpath that will lead you up for a short distance to

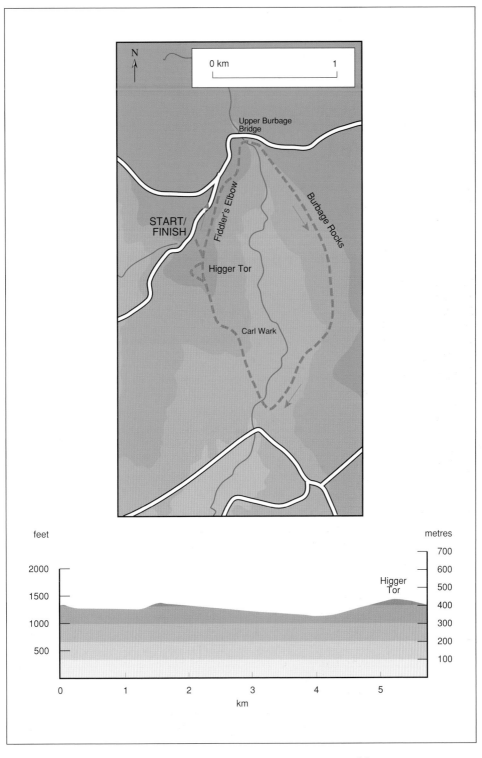

Carl Wark and Higger Tor viewed from the disused quarry near Burbage Bridge.

reach the extensive flat summit of Higger Tor to the s. At an elevation of 434m (1425ft), this area deserves a thorough exploration, for in clear weather the views from here are simply stunning. A few words of warning, however: the steep and sometimes unexpected fall-aways around the edges of Higger Tor are potentially dangerous, and you should therefore exercise appropriate care and keep a tight hold of young children at all times. Walk clockwise around the edge of the rocks to observe in sequence:

E The coniferous forested valley down below on your L, with Burbage Rocks and Moors extending for miles beyond.

s From the southernmost tip, a fine panorama which contains the rocky escarpment of Carl Wark, originally an Iron Age settlement. The more gentle, wooded slopes beyond link this outcrop with the regressive gritstone edges of Froggatt and Curbar and the flat, manicured parklands of Chatsworth, which disappear into the far distance.

w–N Fine views of the Hope Valley, the undulating ridge linking Mam Tor and Lose Hill, the pointed, craggy tor of Win Hill and, nearer to you, the serrated, rocky profile of Stanage Edge and the cluster of boulders in which the Cowper Stone is located. The backcloth for these spectacular landscapes is the dark, forbidding, high plateau of Kinder Scout which stretches for miles, forming the horizon to the NW.

Descend from Higger Tor along the wide, sandy path which leads N towards Fiddler's Elbow. The clear, obvious way tracks parallel to the road over to your L and the walking is almost effortless as the path threads gently downhill between bilberry-, bracken- and heather-covered slopes. The way then rises equally gently to reach the top of a modest outcrop of rocks and boulders. Head N along the obvious continuation way, to converge on the road at two bridges – named Upper Burbage Bridge. These have water channels running beneath them and effectively span Burbage Brook at MR 261830. At the approach to the bridges, do not cross over the stile on your L but instead bear R to cross the stream directly below these man-made structures, making good use of the boulders and rock slabs spanning the watercourses in order to keep your feet dry. You will have to negotiate some eroded ground when crossing over the brook, but there is an obvious and well- used way of doing this.

As you round this elbow at the N tip of the route, you will pass close by a pile of faced boulders which are part of the remnants from the former estate of the Duke of Rutland (or so I was informed by a dry stone waller to whom I chatted at this spot). From here, keep to the wide way, disregarding several narrower paths leading uphill on your L. The correct continuation path tracks s below Burbage Rocks. These fascinating gritstone edges, with their numerous rock falls and boulder fields, extend s from here for about 2.5km (1½ miles), forming an irresistible arc that climbers delight in scaling at numerous points. The rock pitches are small and, with their varying degrees of difficulty, the climbing routes therefore make an ideal training ground for youngsters under the watchful eyes of expert climbers and qualified tutors (the Edale Activity Centre provides such expertise).

Distance is quickly and almost effortlessly gobbled up beneath these interesting rock features, as the fairly level path winds its way s in the shelter of the edge and Higger Tor and Carl Wark slip quietly by on the far side of the valley, over to your R. You will have to cross some boggy areas along here in wet weather, but there are no real problems. The wide way then circles to the R to bring you to the southernmost point of the route at MR 262808. In getting there, ignore several side paths off to the L and then the R. The route approaches the main A625 road but never quite gets there. Ignore a grassy track leading acutely back to the R, then select the next path off on this side, just a few paces further on, to commence the section of the walk leading NNW towards Carl Wark.

The path leads to an interesting crossing of Burbage Brook over boulders, where there are easy and more difficult passages from which to choose, in an area that is eroded and often boggy. On the far side the obvious, sandy continuation path snakes up to reach the pile of rocks, fixed boulders and loose stones that forms the escarpment of Carl Wark, but not before your ingenuity has been tested in avoiding a number of muddy patches. Veer L and scramble between the boulders up to the top, taking care as you go. There are several ways of doing this, which vary in difficulty, and some of them will almost certainly call for the steadying use of your hands. In clear weather, there are fine views from the summit. Most of these will be familiar to you by now, but there is the added attraction of some new perspectives of Higger Tor, just a short distance away to the NNW.

The final part of the route – to stand on top of Higger Tor for a second time – starts by crossing the flat area of grass cupped by weathered boulders to the NW. Then, after inspecting the remains of the Iron Age fortifications, bear R down a narrow, eroded chute which becomes slippery in wet weather. At the bottom of this channel a wide, eroded, sandy way rises directly to the top of Higger Tor, a short distance away to the N. Again there are several routes to the top, so choose one with which you are comfortable and take your time. At the top you will be on familiar ground, and from here you simply retrace your outward steps back to your vehicle.

Climbing on to Higger Tor from the south.

TACKLING THE WALK

CASUAL WALKERS

This is an almost ideal route for walkers who like wide open spaces with a modicum of exposure and opportunities for some easy scrambling, around a circuit which is not too challenging.

FAMILY WALKERS

Youngsters will love this walk, with its continual interest and opportunities to climb up rocks and scramble over boulders. I have seen many very young children among the heathers and boulders of Higger Tor, but because of the potential dangers (see route description) they should only be brought up here on warm, windless days, when you can relax and allow them to enjoy themselves to the full in safety.

STRONG, EXPERIENCED WALKERS

This is a pleasant stroll around an interesting circuit. It can also be included in longer walks from Hathersage and/or combined with routes along Stanage Edge to the NW or from Froggatt Edge to the S.

PLACES OF INTEREST

HIGGER TOR AND CARL WARK

Higger Tor is a fascinating mixture of rock faces, large rounded boulders, stones and heather-covered high ground rising some 2.5km (1½ miles) to the ENE of Hathersage. It is a favourite with the people of nearby Sheffield who come here to marvel at the superb views afforded from here in fine weather.

Carl Wark is an ancient Iron Age settlement about 0.5km (¼ mile) to the S of Higger Tor and comprised of much the same millstone grits. It is another very popular place for walkers and other tourists to include when tracking through the area. Visit these two places in late August or early September, when the purple heathers are usually at their finest.

7 LYME PARK AND BOW STONES

**STARTING/
FINISHING POINT**
Carpark at Lyme
Hall OLM 1: MR
963823

**GRADING
OF WALK**
Easy/straight-
forward

**TIME
ALLOWANCE**
4 hours

DISTANCE
9.2km (5.7 miles)

**TOTAL HEIGHT
GAINED**
210m (690ft)

HIGHEST POINT
Near Sponds Hill
390m (1280ft)

GRADIENTS
Gradual climb to start with, including some steeper sections. Undulating way in the central section of the route, followed by steeper downslopes.

PARKING
Massive coach and carpark, but it still fills up quickly at popular times.

PUBLIC TRANSPORT
Bus route 361 to Lyme Park. Other routes passing the entrance gates along High Lane are 67 and 199.

OVERVIEW/INTEREST
Attractions of the historic house, gardens, parkland and woodland of Lyme Park. Open moorland with fine views. Visit the ancient Bow Stones. Plenty of wildlife and extensive woodland flora.

AMENITIES
Refreshment facilities and toilets adjacent to the main carpark. Further facilities exist within the gardens and parkland of Lyme Park.

FOOTPATHS AND WAYSIGNS
Paths are very good and obvious for most of the way, with virtually no waterlogged areas. Some more demanding sections near and on the top part of the route with narrower, less distinct paths and occasional stretches of boggy ground in wet conditions.

MAKE your way to the information and refreshment kiosk (open 11am to 4.30pm). Continue walking NE to climb up the shallow steps adjacent to the boundary wall of Lyme Hall and Gardens, and continue past the imposing entrance to this historic house. Carry on walking by the perimeter wall, turning L and then R to pass by the stable block. Turn R almost immediately to pass through iron gates and then walk along the wide, gravel-surfaced track as it winds around the buildings and gardens. Pass through a wooden gate next to another iron one and continue around the

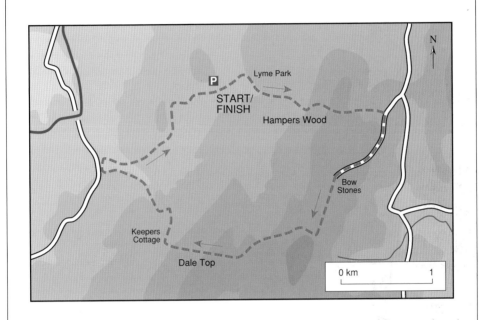

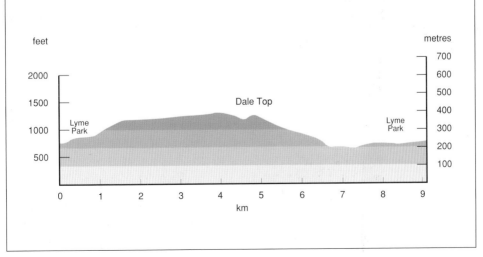

encircling perimeter path, ignoring a way off to the L. Delightful views now open up to your L of lush meadows enclosed by a mixture of mature deciduous trees and rhododendron, with the ground rising gently and uniformly beyond to a tree-fringed horizon of low-lying, rounded, grassy hills.

The obvious way then tracks beside Hampers Wood and you will pass an access gate to the Fallow Deer Sanctuary – this haven is closed to visitors from late May to the end of August to allow the female deer to produce and nurture their young undisturbed. After this the path rises, and further up it leads to a gate and high L-stile over a stone wall which you have to climb. Select the middle of three tracks from here. Your choice is a grassy way which winds further uphill, initially heading SSE but soon curving L, towards the E. There are good views to the rear from this vantage point, including one of the tower of Lyme Cage, below to the NNW.

The grassy cart track then curves back to the high perimeter wall which encloses a group of Scots pine, and you should follow this boundary further up the hillside, ignoring an S-stile over the wall opposite a disused quarry. A rougher, narrow path then leads further up the slope to reach the top of the grassy brow a short distance further on. Just beyond this, a stepped W-stile provides entry to open country. (Be careful climbing over this stile, as there is a steep drop on the far side and the steps are awkwardly positioned.) In good weather there are fantastic views from here of expansive, open countryside, with Black Hill and Whaley Moor to the ENE providing a fine background for the splendidly positioned Moorside Hotel with its manicured grounds.

Continue walking E, now along a narrow but distinct grassy path, and use this to cross a shallow depression in the hillside directly ahead, near the bottom of which the path passes through a tumble-down stone wall. The way rises again to skirt a boggy area and cross an infant watercourse, breaches another dilapidated stone wall and leads over an S-stile, before bringing you to a surfaced lane at another S-stile. Turn R up the lane, disregarding a footpath immediately on the L. Walk along the lane to reach Bow Stones, less than 1km (½ mile) further on to the SW, at MR 974813. As you walk along the lane, more fine views appear on your L of pleasant rural landscapes containing rolling hillsides liberally covered with farms, pastures and clumps of trees. Beyond these the ground rises to the craggy outcrop of Windgather Rocks to the SSE, while further away the ridge on the skyline contains the high ground of Cats Tor and Shining Tor. There is a wooden enclosure at Bow Stones which contains the two stones (see page 61 for details) and access is permitted.

At Bowstonegate, just beyond the stones, walk straight past the two paths leading off to L and R and continue along the walled track, passing through a wooden swing gate to do so. The enclosed way leads ssw along the crest of a broad ridge amid wild moorland scenery, which stretches for miles around in all directions, falling away as it does so. You will cross over a stile, and from here the ground rises slightly to reach another one. In between these two stiles, disregard the footpath on the L signed to 'Whaley Bridge and Kettleshulme'. Then, just over 100 paces beyond the second stile, branch R along a less distinct grassy track which leads to and then along a dry stone wall, also to your R.

Climb over the waysigned s-stile and cross the shallow hause ahead to the W. Branch R again to skirt the higher ground of Dale Top, following the course of the stone wall. You then need to cross two more stiles, the second of these over a wire fence. After this turn full L, keeping to the direction indicated on a Countryside Commission white arrowhead sign. However, immediately beyond a wide gap in the dry stone wall just ahead you should turn R to resume your predominant direction of descent to the W. The grassy path then leads down over Planted Moor towards Keepers Cottage. Turn R when you reach the lane below to pass in front of the attractively located stone cottage with its pretty garden.

About 100 paces further on, climb over the stone wall on your L using the s-stile to continue along the public footpath signed to 'Higher Poynton'. From here, a diagonal way leads slightly downhill across sometimes soggy ground to cross a narrow hawthorn lined, gorse-covered gully, through which a trickle of a watercourse meanders. Climb up the far bank, and then circle to your L

Winter sunshine illuminating Lyme Hall.

Approaching Bow Stones on a crisp winter's day.

around the grassy brow ahead to continue walking downhill. Below, pass through the swing gate and then climb down the steps, which were positioned there fairly recently. The path continues to descend beneath trees to reach a gate-and-stile combination. After negotiating either of these, use the wider track beyond and then the gravel-surfaced lane to reach the road at Shrigley Methodist Chapel, Green Close. Turn R along the road and then R again, to continue along the waysigned public footpath which leads marginally downhill to the N in the form of a wide fenced track.

Ignore a path leading off to the L and cross over a stream via a stone bridge, then turn R to re-enter the grounds of Lyme Park through the imposing West Gate (locked between 8.30pm and 8.00am). From here, a good wide path of compacted stones leads uphill beneath trees and beside the falling watercourse. The dense mixed woodland contains horse chestnut, larch, rowan, 'sycamore and massive clumps of rhododendron, the latter a mass of purple blooms in May and early June. Keep to the obvious main path, avoiding all side paths leading off to L and R. At the top end of the woodland a gate provides access to a small, secluded parking area, and from here a surfaced internal estate road winds down through the parkland to the main carpark near Lyme Hall.

TACKLING THE WALK

CASUAL WALKERS
This route makes a pleasant, not too strenuous half-day ramble for most walkers and, with plenty of interest along the way, you should return to Lyme Park very satisfied with your efforts.

FAMILY WALKERS
Similar remarks apply to family groups, and with many attractions for children in the grounds of Lyme Park the outing should be enjoyed by all families who like to venture into the great outdoors.

STRONG, EXPERIENCED WALKERS
This walk makes a pleasant, leisurely circuit any time you happen to be visiting Lyme Park. The route can also be included as a part of longer, more strenuous walks from more distant starting points such as Disley, High Lane, Higher Poynton and Pott Shrigley.

PLACES OF INTEREST

LYME PARK
The hall, gardens, parkland and extensive woodland of Lyme Park are a major national tourist attraction, with many thousands of people visiting this location each year. The 1996 National Trust leaflet describes Lyme Park as 'one of northern England's great historic houses set in a spectacular moorland park'.

The 1400-acre park supports herds of red and fallow deer, while the gardens extend over 16 acres and include herbaceous borders, a Victorian conservatory, a recently restored Edwardian rose garden and a sunken Dutch garden. The hall traces over 600 years of English history through its architecture and interiors, where different rooms reveal the style of Elizabethan, Stuart, Georgian and Edwardian times. The park was the exterior setting for Pemberley in the recent BBC television adaptation of Jane Austen's *Pride and Prejudice*.

There is a gift and coffee shop in the park located near the banks of a lake, and nearby a children's adventure play area and a miniature golf course.

BOW STONES
Two pillar-like stones standing a couple of metres high are to be found in an accessible fenced-off area at Bow Stones. They are thought to be of Saxon origin and are possibly the bases for crosses. They are also believed to have served originally as landmarks and could well have had some important religious significance.

61

8 PYM CHAIR, CATS TOR, SHINING TOR AND ERRWOOD HALL

**STARTING/
FINISHING POINT**
Carpark at Pym
Chair OLM 24:MR
995768

**GRADING
OF WALK**
Moderate/
challenging

**TIME
ALLOWANCE**
4 hours

DISTANCE
9.4km (5.9 miles)

**TOTAL HEIGHT
GAINED**
350m (1150ft)

HIGHEST POINT
Shining Tor 559m
(1835ft)

GRADIENTS
Moderate climb to the top of Shining Tor. Gradual descent to reach Errwood Hall, followed by another upward traverse below Foxlow Edge.

PARKING
Carpark holds about 25 vehicles, with additional parking in nearby laybys.

PUBLIC TRANSPORT
None.

OVERVIEW/INTEREST
Great variety of scenery and walking terrain. Open moorlands with craggy tors. Sheltered woodland and enclosed pastures. Features the ruins of Errwood Hall.

AMENITIES
No refreshment facilities or toilets *en route*.

FOOTPATHS AND WAYSIGNS
Exposed paths to Shining Tor have been extensively refurbished. From there, paths are mainly good, fairly obvious and well drained. Waysigns are not over-generous.

TURN L out of the carpark along the grassy track at the edge of the side lane and walk up the shallow brow, following the path around to the L. This path hugs the side of the single-track road which is signed to 'Buxton 5', heading NE. At the top of the brow, turn sharp R to cross the road, climb up the bank on the far side and proceed over the S-stile. This provides immediate access to 'Open Country'. In clear weather there are splendid views from here of vast, open landscapes including rugged high moorlands which recede in all directions, together with ranging hills containing regressive escarpments, spurs and craggy edges. When visibility is exceptionally good, the spherical shape of Jodrell Bank Radio

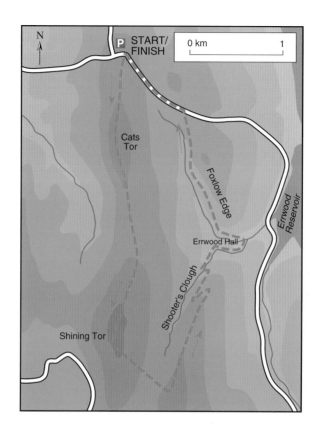

N

P START/
FINISH

0 km   1

Cats
Tor

Foxlow Edge

Errwood Hall

Errwood Reservoir

Shooter's Clough

Shining Tor

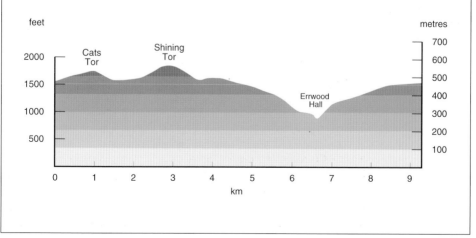

feet

metres

2000

Cats
Tor

Shining
Tor

700

600

500

1500

400

Errwood
Hall

1000

300

200

500

100

0   1   2   3   4   5   6   7   8   9

km

Telescope can be spotted, sticking up out of the flatness of the Cheshire Plain to the w.

The path beyond the stile is signed to 'Shining Tor', your first major objective, about 3km (nearly 2 miles) to the s. Start towards this along the wide path of compacted earth which winds gradually uphill, tracking along the line of a stone wall on your R. As you gain height, you will have clear views to your rear of the climbing pitches of Windgather Rocks, with extensive forested areas stretching below this outcrop to the E along Hoo Moor. Soon your route is along a definite spur and this terrain rises progressively, with shallow undulations taken in your stride along the way. At the top of the next rise, the tors along the ridge you are heading towards come into view, and in the far distance the pointed peak of Shutlingsloe (the Matterhorn of Macclesfield) appears to the ssw.

Following another shallow dip in the ridge, the renovated path leads s to the top of Cats Tor. This refurbished path, a skilful mixture of peat, compacted stones and chippings, is a joy to walk along as it traverses the surrounding ground, which is often waterlogged and extremely boggy after heavy rain. The surrounding moorland flora contains bilberry and hardy grasses. Cross straight over an intersection of ways and carry on uphill to the s along the continuation of your path, which is signed to the 'Cat and Fiddle Inn' on a post dedicated to Sol Almond by the Peak and Northern Footpaths Society on behalf of Buxton Rambling club, and dated 31 July 1985.

The view south west towards Shutlingsloe from the slopes of Shining Tor.

The vast, rounded summit area of Shining Tor is reached a short distance further on. On clear days, the craggy outline of The Roaches may be observed from this elevation of 559m (1835ft), these rocks sticking up due s on the distant horizon. Before continuing, climb over the stile on your R to walk around the flat area surrounding the trig point, to which restricted access is permitted. In doing this, beware of the sheer and potentially dangerous gritstone rock faces which plunge down almost vertically ahead, and keep a tight grip on young children at all times.

Cross back over the stile and then continue SE along a wide path of chippings, again waysigned to the 'Cat and Fiddle'. The next section of the route crosses a wide, shallow depression and as you descend the Cat and Fiddle Inn can be seen ahead, over to the R towards the s. The path then leads uphill to a wooden gate and w-stile. Turn L on the far side of these, to walk along a grassy path that descends towards the woodlands surrounding Errwood and is waysigned as part of local walk 1. Your changed direction is now towards the N. Further down, the s end of the Errwood/Fernilee Reservoir complex appears below on your R, to the NNE. Continue walking downhill over bilberry- and heather-covered slopes in the general direction of the water.

The path leads between redundant stone pillars marking a former gateway and you will then reach a division of ways. Turn L here to mount the tall L-stile, which provides access to your continuation way along a path signed to 'Errwood Hall'. This path traverses down sw into an attractive wooded valley of mixed conifers and deciduous trees including spruce, Scots pine, oak and sycamore. Note that flies can be a nuisance when walking along here during the summer months. Just past another disused gateway turn acutely R, following waysigned trail 1a to continue your descent into the recesses of Shooter's Clough. The signed, grassy path continues to zigzag down the wooded slope in a series of traverses, to reach a patch of rhododendron bushes below.

Continue walking downhill until you reach a wider cart track ahead. Turn R here and follow the walled track down towards the grounds of Errwood Hall – now a ruin – walking along a pleasant sheltered, tree-lined valley. Within a short distance, bear off L along the way which leads between two unusual and imposing square stone pillars. The way down then passes beneath more trees and over steps; ignore the the rougher side paths leading off to the L. Your descent continues along grassy sections interspersed with flights of stone steps, and this combination will lead you to the impressive remains of Errwood Hall.

After examining this interesting assortment of faced stone blocks and the foundations of the hall, continue around to the L to walk uphill once more along another, not dissimilar, deep-sided,

*A figurine inside
the moorland
shrine near
Errwood Hall.*

narrow wooded valley, climbing w through more rhododendron bushes. The way then descends to cross a stream (which eventually flows into Errwood Reservoir) by means of stepping stones. Above this crossing, keep walking straight ahead, now following local walk 2 uphill; do not turn off to either l or r along the intersecting path.

A rougher path now leads n up a grassy incline. Further up the clough be careful to keep to the main track (local walk 2), avoiding a well-used side path on your r, waysigned 2a. The path continues to gain height gradually and leads you above another wide, densely forested valley along the lower flank of Foxlow Edge, high above to your r. Further up, the path clips a group of trees, which on hot sunny days provide a conflicting mixture of welcome shade and annoying flies. The uphill gradient eventually levels off near a dilapidated stone building to your r. Just past this rubble, be careful to branch off to your l along a narrow side path, which leads down to a round stone building with narrow slits in its walls and a cross on top of its conical roof. Open the door to observe the shrine (see page 67) – and perhaps even to translate the following words:

*Nunca Se le
Invoca Envano
A San José
Prueba de Gratitud D de Y
1889*

Climb back to the main path up the stone steps located on the far side of the shrine, and then veer l along this path at the top to continue your walk n. The path connects with the minor road a short distance further on at MR 002761 (in reaching this point you will have avoided branching R along another side path waysigned 2a). Climb over the S-stile, cross over the road at the layby and turn L along the raised footpath on the far side. You will soon be heading NW towards the brow of the hill ahead. From the top of this, retrace your outward steps back to the carpark just below, off to the R, ignoring a path off to the R along the ridge signed to 'Windgather Rocks'.

TACKLING THE WALK

CASUAL WALKERS
This is a splendid outing for casual walkers: the spice of walking across high moorlands and climbing up exposed tors is followed by exploring the more sheltered grounds and remains of Errwood Hall.

FAMILY WALKERS
The walk should also appeal to most family groups, and if you tackle the uphill sections at a pace which is comfortable for the children everyone should have an enjoyable day out. However, those with very young children are advised to drive down to the carpark and picnic area near Errwood Reservoir at MR 012748, and to keep to the forest trails in this vicinity.

STRONG, EXPERIENCED WALKERS
The first part of this route should be relished by dedicated walkers. The circuit is easily extended by walking down to and then along the reservoirs, before returning by way of Overton Hall Farm and Windgather Rocks.

PLACES OF INTEREST

CATS TOR AND SHINING TOR
These are two mounds of harder gritstones rising along a continuous ridge to the SW of the Goyt Valley. At 559m (1835ft), Shining Tor is the higher of the two, and with its exposed rock faces and boulder fields is by far the more impressive.

ERRWOOD HALL
All that remains of Errwood Hall today are its foundations and a pile of large, faced, stone building blocks. The house was constructed in the early nineteenth century and was the home of the Grimshawe family. On the moorlands above is a circular stone building put up in 1889 as a shrine to a Miss Dolores, a Spanish lady who was both a companion to Mrs Grimshawe and governess to the children.

9 MACCLESFIELD FOREST AND SHUTLINGSLOE

STARTING/ FINISHING POINT
Carpark at Trentabank Reservoir OLM 24: MR 961711

GRADING OF WALK
Moderate/ challenging

TIME ALLOWANCE
3 hours

DISTANCE
6.2km (3.8 miles)

TOTAL HEIGHT GAINED
250m (820ft)

HIGHEST POINT
Shutlingsloe 506m (1660ft)

GRADIENTS
Steady pull up to the top of Shutlingsloe with some steep sections, particularly the final assault. Descent is more spread out.

PARKING
Attractively positioned carpark holds about 25 cars, but is very popular.

PUBLIC TRANSPORT
None.

OVERVIEW/INTEREST
Forests and reservoirs with plenty of bird life, including herons. Also high moorland terrain with a craggy tor. Magnificent views above the tree line. Plenty of interesting features for children.

AMENITIES
Toilets and information point at the carpark, but no further facilities *en route*. Colourful free leaflets available outside the carpark building describing the various forest walks.

FOOTPATHS AND WAYSIGNS
Paths are good to excellent, with splendid upgrading work commissioned by North West Water. Few boggy or wet areas. Entire route is fairly obvious and few signs are needed – but plenty are provided.

FROM the side of the information and toilet block, walk E along the broad, tree-lined path following the sign for 'Forest walks 1, 2 and 3'. Within 100 paces you will pass through a wooden gate and should bear R along a forest road, but when this bends sharply R, turn off along the short connecting path on the L to reach the main path leading uphill into Macclesfield Forest. Turn R up this, walking SE to reach an intersection of paths above. Disregard the concession bridleway off to the R to continue along the main path, which is signed 'Shutlingsloe: Standing Stone, 2 and 3'. After a fairly level stretch, the way steepens again as it tracks up the hillside beneath conifers.

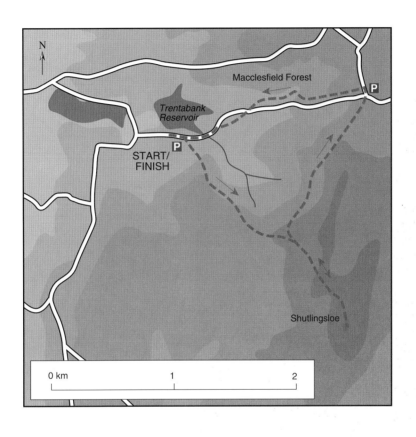

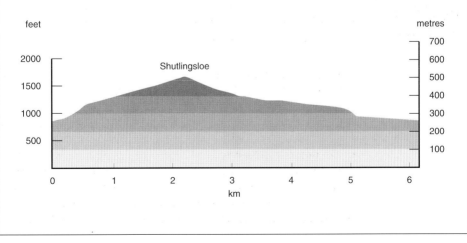

Further up, fork R along the narrower path, again waysigned to 'Shutlingsloe'. The way leads past a recently positioned memorial bench dedicated to Fred Lawton 1918–1995 (no relation) by Congleton Autumnal Amblers. A short distance beyond this seat the way reaches the edge of the forest, which you should leave over an S-stile to access open moorland and the paved continuation path signed to 'Wildboarclough via Shutlingsloe'. Moving into the open, the first clear views of the expansive hilly landscapes appear ahead to your R. This high terrain houses the telecommunications aerials on Croker Hill, and these can be identified on the horizon to the SW.

You will quickly reach the higher ground of the ridge ahead and along here the first sightings of the impressive conical helmet of Shutlingsloe appear, consisting of a jumbled mound of gritstones and sandstones silhouetted against the skyline to the S. A wooden causeway conveniently spans a treacherous waterlogged section and you then climb over a stile and turn immediately R to walk along an impressive flagged way next to a stone wall on the R. The route then leads to a formidably high stone wall, over which an S-stile has been placed. Stone steps wind up from the far side of this obstacle to the top of the tor. Just below the summit, erosion control diverts the approach around to the R before the large, flattish summit area is gained.

The top of Shutlingsloe commands a height of 506m (1660ft) and in fine weather the panoramic views from this platform are superb. Black Hill lies far away to the N; Cats Tor and Shining Tor are nearer, to the NE; Axe Edge, Oliver Hill, Ramshaw Rocks and The Roaches come into view when turning further E; Tittesworth Reservoir occupies the low ground to the SE; Gun Hill rises to the S; Mow Cop, Bosley Cloud and Croker Hill occupy the skyline to the SW; and finally Tegg's Nose rises above your direction of approach to the NE. An illustrated compass set in a rock face near the trig point will help you to identify and position all these features.

Descend, retracing your outward steps back to the fringe of the forest and climb over the S-stile once again. Within the trees, fork almost immediately R and walk down through the pine and spruce, using a narrow connecting path to reach the broad track below, along which you then turn R to continue NE. The way, which is also used by forest walks 2 and 3, descends gradually for some distance. Then a pleasant elevated, terraced way winds at a fairly constant height across more densely forested slopes. When the forest walks bend to the L to descend more rapidly, turn off R to mount the wooden steps and then continue along a grassy path which rises ahead through a clearing in the trees.

The way leads between two redundant gateposts and the path

then bears R, keeping to the more open ground. Cross the brow of the hill ahead and the grassy path then leads gradually back downhill. Continue walking NE as the path descends, to reconnect with the wider forest track below opposite a small, muddy pool. From here, the continuation way leads along the E perimeter of the forest, and this circles around progressively to your L to lead you to the junction of roads at MR 978714. Leave this intersection by the road signed 'Macclesfield Forest ½: Macclesfield 5: Buxton 7', along which forest walks 2 and 3 also lead. However, within 40 paces you should turn off L to follow the signed continuation of the two forest walks, passing through a swing gate to avoid having to cross a cattle grid.

You will now pass Standing Stone carpark on your L. Here you are reasonably requested to keep to the waysigned paths while walking through the forests. Do so by veering L, following the direction indicated by the marker posts. Your way, and forest walk 2, then track downhill to the W along a grassy path to thread through further redundant gateposts. This section is along a usually dry, well-drained way covered with a carpet of decomposing pine needles, twigs and other forest debris. Further down the wooded slope you will reach a wider forest track. Turn R along this in the direction opposite to the nearby road, keeping to the route signed for forest walk 2.

About 100 paces further on you will reach a small, fenced-off pool on your R. Be careful to turn off L opposite this to continue along the path signed to 'Trentabank' which forest walk 2 also

Walkers on the summit of a frosty Shutlingsloe.

71

follows (the way directly ahead leads off-course to Forest Chapel). After taking a few strides uphill, turn L again to continue descending, still in the company of forest walk 2. From here a wide sandy way leads further downhill, using recently refurbished steps and raised duckboards spanning a narrow brook to reach the roadway below at an S-stile. Cross over and walk down the continuation path on the far side. This is accessed by passing through a G-stile in a dry stone wall.

The way down then crosses over two converging water channels which feed the reservoirs below, and there is a cautionary sign here which reads 'This is drinking water, do not pollute'. You will go up and down steps and re-cross the trickling stream, before the tastefully constructed way leads through a narrow G-stile back to the road again. Bear L along this to walk the short remaining distance back to the carpark, using the path along the opposite edge of the road to achieve this. The final approach passes by the E tip of Trentabank Reservoir, and if you look across the placid waters you should be able to spot nesting grey herons, which have colonized the tops of tall trees on the far bank of the reservoir. There is a particularly good viewing point down on the R, just before you cross the road again to re-enter the carpark.

The nature reserve at Trentabank Reservoir.

TACKLING THE WALK

CASUAL WALKERS

This is an ideal outing for casual walkers, with contrasting sheltered forests and exposed moorlands rising to a famous tor.

FAMILY WALKERS

Standing on the summit of Shutlingsloe is enjoyed by many family groups and I have even seen numbers of tiny tots up there. If the climb proves too hard for the children, simply revert to exploring one or more of the delightful, well-marked trails circling through Macclesfield Forest.

STRONG, EXPERIENCED WALKERS

Most people who enjoy walking in the Peak District will climb Shutlingsloe. The short walk described makes a delightful evening stroll, particularly on a warm summer's day. Alternatively, the route is easily extended by dropping down to the Crag Inn in Wildboarclough and then either retracing your steps or completing a longer, more demanding circuit which takes in the Wild Boar Inn as well!

PLACES OF INTEREST

MACCLESFIELD FOREST AND TRENTABANK WILDLIFE RESERVE

Macclesfield Forest occupies a large, almost circular area on rising ground to the ESE of the town of Macclesfield. The forest is very popular with visitors, and North West Water and the other authorities involved have done much to provide admirable recreational facilities, including waysigned forest walks, and to encourage environmentally friendly activities such as bird watching. The important heronry at Trentabank Reservoir is the largest in the Peak National Park, and Cheshire Wildlife Trust protects the grey heron and numerous other species of birds which are attracted to this sanctuary (and detailed on an informative noticeboard).

SHUTLINGSLOE

This famous craggy tor rises to 506m (1660ft) to the SE of Macclesfield Forest. It is a fairly isolated peak and its pointed shape, visible for miles around in fine weather, has earned it the nickname of 'the Matterhorn of Macclesfield'. It is a firm favourite with local walkers and there is usually standing room only on its popular summit on bank holidays, including Boxing Day and New Year's Day – particularly when it is covered in snow.

10 THE ROACHES, LUD'S CHURCH (CAVE) AND HANGING STONE

STARTING/ FINISHING POINT
Layby below The Roaches OLM 24: 004622

GRADING OF WALK
Moderate/ challenging

TIME ALLOWANCE
5 hours

DISTANCE
11km (6.9 miles)

TOTAL HEIGHT GAINED
350m (1150ft)

HIGHEST POINT
The Roaches (trig point) 505m (1655ft)

GRADIENTS

Short, sharp climb to the top of The Roaches. More ups and downs after this but nothing really strenuous.

PARKING

Space for about 25 cars by the roadside, with reserved section for the disabled and a turning area. Additional parking at nearby Tittesworth Reservoir, Meerbrook (MR 994603), with park-and-ride bus service (221) to The Roaches at weekends and on bank holidays.

PUBLIC TRANSPORT

No other bus service.

OVERVIEW/INTEREST

Superb ridge affording fine views among spectacular moorland scenery. Fantastic rock features and exposed rock faces. Opportunity to observe climbers at close quarters. Features Lud's Church (cave) and Hanging Stone (rocks). Animal and bird life in abundance, including wallabies.

AMENITIES

No toilets or refreshment facilities *en route*, and these are therefore unavailable unless you start from Tittesworth Reservoir and use the park-and-ride service.

FOOTPATHS AND WAYSIGNS

Paths and the ways through the rocks are clear and usually well drained, and renovated footpaths are in good condition. Signs are usually there when needed.

THE walk commences amid spectacular moorland scenery with the vast, wooded landscapes of the Staffordshire plain receding for miles below into a bluish haze in the sw, embracing the indented shape of Tittesworth Reservoir. To the s the craggy hill of Hen Cloud rises like a proud sentinel, while over to the e the jumble of rock faces and gigantic boulders which form The Roaches rise above, beyond the grassy slopes linking these with

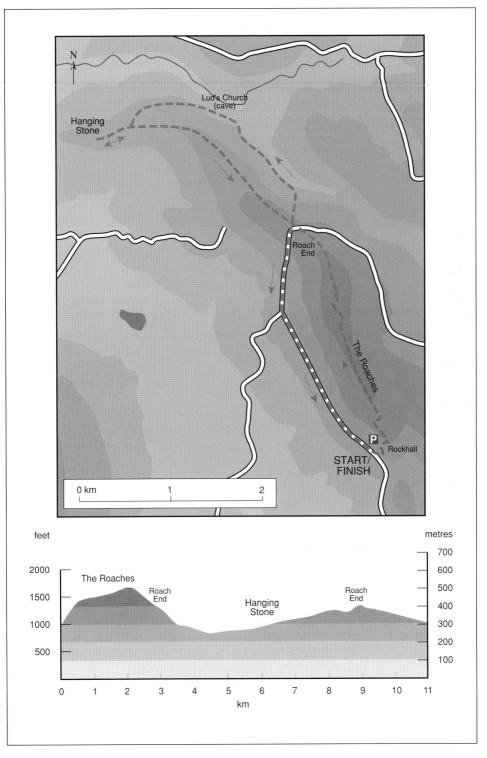

N

Lud's Church
(cave)

Hanging
Stone

Roach
End

The Roaches

P

Rockhall

START/
FINISH

| 0 km | 1 | 2 |

feet

metres

2000

1500

1000

500

The Roaches

Roach
End

Hanging
Stone

Roach
End

700
600
500
400
300
200
100

0 1 2 3 4 5 6 7 8 9 10 11
km

the car layby. Set off sse down the road in the direction of Hen Cloud and then turn off L to enter The Roaches Estate through the wooden gate at the lower end of the parking area.

Veer L and walk uphill along the wide gravel path, ignoring another path that leads off more acutely to your L. Your direction will change to E. Turn L up the next, stepped path which leads more directly to the seductive rock faces and edges of The Roaches. Your path merges with another and here you will need to bear L to pass by Rockhall Cottage (Don Whillan's Memorial Hut) positioned above on the R. Then branch R to pass through a convenient gap in the stone wall ahead and climb uphill through pine and larch trees, heading NE towards the vertical rock faces directly above. Fortunately, these rock faces do not have to be scaled on this walk! Instead, locate the flight of stone steps which provides a relatively easy way up for walkers to the top of these awesome climbing pitches with their technically extremely severe overhangs.

The steps thread up a secure way between the rock faces and boulders, with virtually no exposure. You will emerge into more open terrain at the top, where there are revealing views of other rock faces higher above, as well as vistas of more distant features such as Hen Cloud, which reappears to the se. Now turn L to follow the rough, boulder-strewn path which leads N, gaining marginal height as it passes more formidable, overhanging rock faces. These are often occupied by climbers, clinging to their precarious hand- and footholds, deciding what their next move should be!

The well-used path leads beneath another group of mixed Scots pine and larch to bring you to the fringe of a nature reserve, where the continuation path has been re-routed upwards to the R. Here, a rough, signed way threads up the bilberry-covered slopes to deposit you on the higher level of The Roaches escarpment. Branch L at the top of this to continue N along the edge of the interesting rock configurations, following an obvious path which runs beside a low dry stone wall; keep this to your L as you walk further uphill. The superb surrounding scenery is extended when you reach the top of the next rise where, in clear weather, the escarpment of Bosley Cloud comes into view to the wnw. Then quite unexpectedly the hidden dark, peaty waters of tiny Doxey Pool appear to your R, providing an almost perfect foreground for your camera shots of the surrounding wild landscapes.

From the pool, the broad, compacted way leads further N, hugging the precipitous edges which are always nearby on your L, to reach the highest point along The Roaches ridge. This is marked by a trig point and stands at a height of 505m (1655ft), located at MR 001639. On the way there, avoid the concession footpath leading off across the moorland on your R. Most of the superb moorland scenery which can be viewed from this high spot in favourable weather has already been positioned, but from this vantage point there are extended views to the N, including the fine, pointed tor of Shutlingsloe to the NNW.

Continue tracking N down the wide, obvious path, passing more fantastic rock shapes and quite quickly reaching the narrow road below. Cross over and climb the steps leading to a narrow gap in the dry stone wall on the other side. Squeeze through this and then turn immediately R to use an S-stile, which provides access to the grassy path leading downhill to the N towards woodland below. Follow the path signed with a yellow arrowhead as it meanders through heathers, bilberry and bracken next to a dry stone wall on your R. The way down becomes rougher as it curves L to enter the deciduous woodland, and at the bottom of the slope it crosses a tiny watercourse. Continue up the brow ahead and then turn full L to follow the path signed to 'Lud's Church' along a changed direction towards the W.

The route continues along an elevated, undulating path, tracking close to the upper edge of the wooded area on your L. The path leads over a carpet of pine needles to the top of a narrow cave known as Lud's Church. Take a signed turn to the L, away from the continuation path towards Swythamley, then veer R to avoid a concession path to the L leading up to the ridge above, in order to get into position above the entrance to the extensive cave system of narrow passageways. Avoid the erosion control area to the R and descend into the darker recesses of the cave, climbing down the stone steps by the side of the gorge-like, perpendicular rock faces. Keep to the obvious, natural route through the passageways between the wet rocks, which are host to bracken, lichen and mosses, in this damp, dark environment. The exit is up more stone steps that wind to the L.

Walk out into full daylight once again, and a short distance further on the continuation route will pass close to an interesting assortment of red rocks over on your R, near to the edge of the extensive woodland. At this point keep to the path signed to 'Swythamley', disregarding the turning off back to your R which leads to 'Gradbach'. A slight upwards incline follows as the path curves progressively around to the L through copious bilberry and heathers, to reach an intersection of ways at MR 977655. Climb over the S-stile adjacent to the wooden gate, and about 50 paces further on turn R over the awkwardly positioned and complicated crossing of a dry stone wall and adjacent fence, beginning by using the S-stile.

Bear L along the grassy ridge, locating and following a faint path of sorts which threads between clumps of juncus grass. Cross another fence and dry stone wall by means of an L-stile, and then

*The silhouette
of The Roaches
viewed across
Tittesworth
Reservoir.*

continue w towards the crest of the grassy brow along a better-defined path. This converges on another dry stone wall on your L and then passes through a gap in it, to deposit you directly above the huge slab of rock aptly named Hanging Stone. Descend carefully and walk around the stone to inspect it from all angles, and to read the interesting dedication displayed on a plaque located near its base in memory of Lt Col Henry Courtney Brocklehurst of the 10th Hussars, Game Warden of the Sudan, who was born at nearby Swythamley and was killed on active service in Burma in 1942.

Afterwards, retrace your steps back to the junction of ways at MR 977655. Here, after using the s-stile for a second time, turn immediately R to follow the rising path signed to 'Roach End'. This path leads E along the sweeping ridge, passing through more ground cover of mixed bilberry and heathers. Cross over several more s-stiles and ignore a path crossing at right angles, which connects Cloughhead with Lud's Church, and another signed to 'Danebridge', before reaching the minor road again at Roach End. The final approach to this is by the side of a dry stone wall on your R and then over an s-stile, until eventually you will repeat the squeeze through the narrow G-stile to bring you out on the road again. This time, turn R down the lane, cross over an s-stile positioned near a gate, and then use this surfaced way to return to your vehicle some 3km (1¾ miles) further s, passing through another metal gate on the way.

TACKLING THE WALK

CASUAL WALKERS
The suggested route should appeal to all casual walkers, providing them with good experience and perhaps a taste for more adventurous walks.

FAMILY WALKERS
Although I have seen young children scrambling around on The Roaches, it is an area full of potential dangers and they need to be under constant supervision while up there. The route is definitely not one for tiny tots, who will probably enjoy an outing to Tittesworth Reservoir and a short walk around the village of Meerbrook much more.

STRONG, EXPERIENCED WALKERS
The Roaches are challenging ground for walkers of most abilities and the suggested route has many interesting features along the way. Serious walkers may like to tackle some of the alternative ways up and down the rocks, and might also consider including

Climbers testing their skills on the rock faces of The Roaches.

a climb up Hen Cloud. In addition, looking at maps of the area will show that the route can be extended in a number of other ways.

PLACES OF INTEREST

THE ROACHES

The Roaches are a superb example of an area of upthrust sandstone and gritstone containing an assortment of vertical rock faces, weathered boulders and other fascinating rock features. The Peak National Park Authority, which manages The Roaches Estate, encourages the coexistence of recreational activities such as climbing and walking and the preservation of a reserve in which wildlife may flourish and multiply. Walls have been restored, paths renovated and concession ways negotiated which provide access to many popular features in the immediate vicinity, including Lud's Church and the Hanging Stone.

LUD'S CHURCH

This is a natural cave and not, as the name implies, a man-made feature. The crevasse was formed by a lateral fault in the gritstone bedding planes and the movement of softer clays beneath. The rocks are now stable and safe to walk through and explore. The cave is a candidate for the legendary Green Chapel alluded to in the poem *Sir Gawain and the Green Knight*. More probably, as the present name suggests, the hidden retreat was used as a refuge for worship and religious ceremonies, and the location is associated with the Lollards – followers of the zealous reformer John Wycliffe.

81

11 CURBAR EDGE, EAGLE STONE AND WELLINGTON'S MONUMENT

STARTING/ FINISHING POINT
Carpark above Curbar OLM 24: MR 262747

GRADING OF WALK
Easy/straight-forward

TIME ALLOWANCE
2½ hours

DISTANCE
6.3km (3.9 miles)

TOTAL HEIGHT GAINED
100m (330ft)

HIGHEST POINT
Along Curbar Edge 330m (1085ft)

GRADIENTS
Steepish descent from Curbar Edge, followed by a more gradual climb back.

PARKING
Carpark holds up to 40 cars in several separate bays.

PUBLIC TRANSPORT
None, although there are numerous bus services to nearby Calver.

OVERVIEW/INTEREST
Fine start in open country beside Curbar Edge. Features rock pitches with a multitude of climbing routes below. Some walking through sheltered, deciduous woodland. Visit the Eagle Stone and Wellington's Monument.

AMENITIES
No refreshment facilities or toilets directly available on the walk, but the Bridge Inn in the village of Curbar/Calver below offers both. Larger conurbation of Baslow nearby has additional amenities and attractions, including gateways to Chatsworth Park.

FOOTPATHS AND WAYSIGNS
Paths generally good to excellent, obvious and mostly well drained. Navigation relatively complicated in some places. Signs vary: a few more at strategic turnings would be helpful.

Fʀᴏᴍ the front parking level, head up the steps along the path signed to 'Curbar Edge'. This precipitous fall-away is located a short distance to the w and is reached through a ᴋ-gate which provides immediate access to the Eastern Moors Estate. Branch ʟ along the grassy path that leads to the spectacular edges, walking ᴡɴᴡ across heather-covered moorland to get to them. In favourable weather, the views from these gritstone edges are simply stunning. The attractively positioned twin villages of Curbar and

82

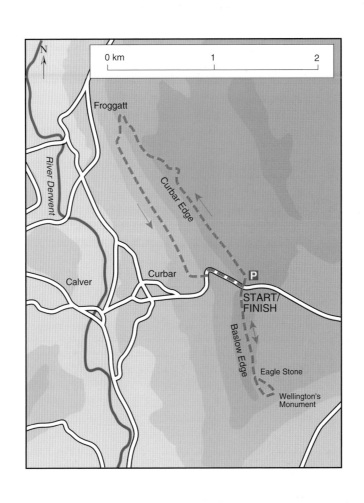

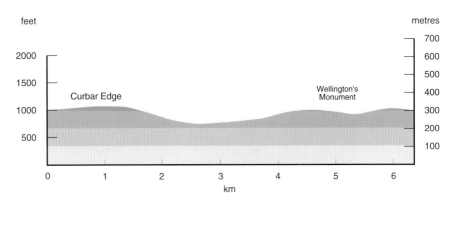

Calver are spread out directly below to the w, while further away to the wnw the buildings of Stoney Middleton may be observed at the entrance to the rocky cleft of Middleton Dale. Surrounding these three villages are vast, rural landscapes consisting of low, rounded hills and tree-lined valleys with orderly farms and pastures, with the powerful River Derwent meandering lazily through this scene of rare natural beauty.

To your R the gritstone edges beckon, so turn that way and walk along them to continue N, threading your way through the random boulders spread about close to the brim of the rock pitches. In secure places you may peer over the edges to observe the many challenging climbing routes – perhaps with experts in position on them – which link the benign lower, wooded slopes with your safe position on top. A warning, however: refrain from doing this when it is either very windy or icy underfoot, and always keep a firm, restraining hold on young children while near these potentially dangerous drops.

More vast landscapes are revealed as you track N along the edges, including the continuation gritstone edges which partly encircle the village of Hathersage. Continue on towards these distant vistas, choosing to be led by either the main wide, compressed path or the more adventurous side paths nearer to the plunging, precipitous drops. Some distance further on, the terrain begins to descend gently as the buildings of Froggatt appear ahead in the valley below, and you will pass by a group of hardy silver birch trees.

The main path then loops decisively to the R and a wooden marker post is located at this point (MR 251763). This marks the start of a branch path on the L, which you need to follow as it tracks downwards beneath the rock faces. The sandy path weaves below awesome cliff faces which are often speckled with climbers

Looking south along Curbar Edge.

demonstrating their considerable skills. Then be vigilant to turn sharp L away from the plunging rock pitches, to follow a rough, stony path which leads steeply downhill on a surface which is initially loose. This tricky ground improves lower down to become a firmer, more secure path of compacted earth as the route passes through dense woodland.

Just before you reach a wall and stile, turn off L along a grassy track which leads S on a fairly level traverse. Climb over the W-stile ahead, positioned near a green-painted iron gate, to continue walking beneath the trees along a level way. Cross over a second stile and then keep to the obvious main path, ignoring a side path leading down on the R. Beyond this you will reach more open terrain, where you may catch glimpses of the fascinating serrated skyline of Curbar Edge, which is now high above to your L. Further on, the continuing escarpment of Baslow Edge also comes into view towards the S.

When the path eventually reaches a stone wall on your R, do not pass through the iron gate but instead opt to continue along the narrow path to the L. This threads through dense bracken to lead you to an L-stile over a stone wall. Now turn immediately L to avoid trespassing into private land straight ahead. From here a faint, grassy path leads uphill beside a dry stone wall on your L. The path then passes through a gap in another stone wall running at right angles to your direction of approach. The continuation way then tracks under the low, spreading boughs of sycamore trees to continue E uphill, passing through a G-stile at the corner of dry stone walling – be careful not to bear R at the trees along a track which resembles a path but which is not a right of way.

Cross the next small field on an upwards diagonal to your R, to pass over another stile which provides access to the road. Turn L along it and follow the hairpin bends ahead towards Curbar Gap, passing by the entrance to Warren Lodge Farmhouse, which offers bed and breakfast. Avoid all paths leading off to L and R until you near the carpark at the top of the brow, where you should branch off R up a wide, stone- and gravel-surfaced path to pass through a wooden gate in a cluster of three. This provides entry to another part of the Eastern Moors Estate, on this occasion enabling you to walk S along Baslow Edge in order to visit the Eagle Stone and Wellington's Monument.

These two isolated attractions are reached along obvious, well-used paths and a triangular route can be used to visit them in turn without retracing your steps unnecessarily. Walk first to the Eagle Stone, which is located at MR 263738, and from there proceed to the nearby Wellington's Monument at MR 264737. On the way, in favourable weather there are fine views further S, down on your R, towards the lush parklands of Chatsworth, with the River Derwent meandering placidly through them; the house is also visible from here. The Eagle Stone is a gigantic boulder which is a challenge to climb, and the monument a fine stone obelisk dedicated to the great soldier (see page 87).

Afterwards, walk back to the entrance gates at the edge of the estate, pass through one of them, turn R by the side of the road and return to the carpark which is just above.

TACKLING THE WALK

CASUAL WALKERS

This is a delightful route which should appeal to casual walkers. It is far from strenuous but is still full of interest, and there is the added attraction of peering over precipitous edges from safe, flat vantage points!

FAMILY WALKERS

Similar remarks apply to family groups, although you should take great care of children when near the potentially dangerous edges. Should you not wish to descend into the valley along the steep and initially rough path, simply retrace your outward steps back along Curbar Edge, taking in any views that you may have missed on the way out.

STRONG, EXPERIENCED WALKERS

The route may be extended easily to the N or S either by walking along Froggatt Edge or venturing to Gardom Edge – real enthusiasts may consider doing both! There are also several longer return routes involving descending to and then walking along the River Derwent.

PLACES OF INTEREST

CURBAR EDGE

Curbar Edge is a spectacular gritstone cliff overlooking the River Derwent at the W lip of Big Moor. It is part of a massive series of rocky edges which stretch roughly N–S for many kilometres and include Stanage Edge, Burbage Rocks, Froggatt Edge, Curbar Edge, Baslow Edge, Gardom Edge and Dobb Edge. These challenging rock faces are a Mecca for climbers in the area and offer several hundred recognized routes of varying severity.

EAGLE STONE

This is a gigantic, erratic boulder, 4.3m (14ft) high and weighing many tonnes, which was left by the retreating ice fields when the region was covered by glaciers. The stone has several bevelled

A young climber on 'trapeze direct' under the watchful eyes of instructors.

protrusions which make it particularly difficult to get to the top. It does, however, provide welcome shade for highland cattle in the hot summer months!

WELLINGTON'S MONUMENT

Situated quite close to the Eagle Stone, this monument, in the shape of a stone cross, stands about 3m (10ft) high and was built in 1866 in memory of the Duke of Wellington 1769–1852. It was erected on the initiative of a Baslow antiquarian, who as a young man had served in the Duke's Regiment: he thought that the Nelson's Monument on Birchen Edge, across the valley, ought to have a mate!

THE
WHITE PEAK

12 CASTLETON, CAVE DALE AND THE WINNATS PASS

STARTING/ FINISHING POINT
Carpark in Castleton centre OLM 1: MR 149829

GRADING OF WALK
Easy/straight-forward

TIME ALLOWANCE
3½ hours

DISTANCE
7.4km (4.6 miles)

TOTAL HEIGHT GAINED
270m (885ft)

HIGHEST POINT
Near Slitherstone Mine (disused) 470m (1540ft)

GRADIENTS
Gradual climb up Cave Dale, with some steeper sections. Downhill for most of the remainder of the way.

PARKING
Large, well-appointed coach and carpark.

PUBLIC TRANSPORT
Extensive bus services from many areas, including nearby villages and more distant towns and cities such as Manchester, Sheffield and Huddersfield.

OVERVIEW/INTEREST
Starts from the attractive major tourist centre of Castleton. Superb, ever-changing scenery, including limestone gorges and open moorland. Features Peveril Castle and nearby limestone caverns and mines. Opportunity to examine fossils, including crinoids.

AMENITIES
Toilets at the carpark. Refreshments and other amenities available in the busy tourist village of Castleton.

FOOTPATHS AND WAYSIGNS
Paths are usually clear, with adequate signs at most turnings. Going is good for much of the way, with a few sections where water accumulates, making the ground heavy and muddy. Few exceptions should not present any real problems.

Previous pages: Looking along wooded Miller's Dale towards Cressbrook.

TURN L out of the carpark, heading along the main road into the centre of the village. Immediately you will observe that the walls of Peveril Castle dominate the steeply rising, rounded green hillsides overlooking Castleton. Turn first R along Castle Street to pass by the rear of the parish church of St Edmund on your L. When you reach the youth hostel, veer L uphill along Market Place, passing by the poignant war memorial triangle on

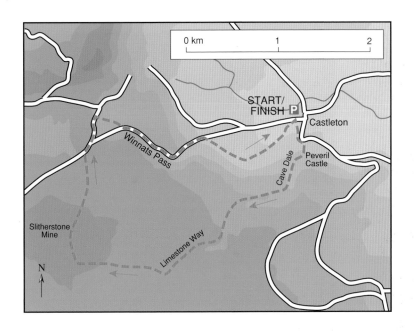

0 km   1   2

START/
FINISH P

Castleton

Winnats Pass

Cave Dale

Peveril
Castle

Slitherstone
Mine

Limestone Way

N

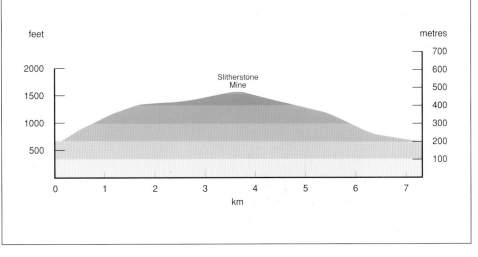

feet   metres

                                                                        700
2000   600
                                         Slitherstone   500
                                            Mine
1500   400

                                                                        300
1000
                                                                        200
 500
                                                                        100

    0   1   2   3   4   5   6   7
                            km

your L. Continue along Pindale Road, and when the road bears L, turn off to the R along the signed Limestone Way to enter the limestone gorge of Cave Dale. You will pass by Cavedale Cottage as you proceed uphill along a broad, surfaced pathway.

A gate-and-stile combination bars the entrance to the gorge, and as you proceed you are warned of loose rocks on the sides of the dale. From here a rougher, stony path leads uphill through a spectacular setting of steep, interlaced limestone cliffs, where the sweeping grassy areas are savagely punctured by sharply pointed

limestone tors and columns. Exposed cliff faces, loose scree and dark caves add to the overall grandeur of this fascinating scene. The obvious continuation way, along a narrow path, winds uphill along a deepening chasm. With so much of interest to hold your attention, you will hardly notice the uphill gradient and will make rapid and almost effortless progress along the rising dale.

Further on, the fortifications of Peveril Castle dominate the R flank of the dale from their almost impregnable position, perched on top of a near-vertical limestone cliff face. The route bears L,

Peveril Castle overlooking a snow-covered Cave Dale.

following the contours of the cleft to gain further height along the well-trodden way, which contorts s to penetrate the narrowing jaws of the upper reaches of the dale. Look around here at a particularly fine view back along the chasm towards Castleton and the Mam Tor to Lose Hill ridge which protects the N flank of the Hope Valley, now far below.

The stony path snakes between converging limestone cliffs before winding further uphill as it seeks out the head of the dale, still some distance away. Along here more revealing views open up of the landscapes behind you, and from this higher elevation the pointed summit of Lose Hill may be spotted in clear weather rising to the NNE above Peveril Castle. The path then leads to a wooden gate in a stone wall, which you should pass through. From near here, along a short diversion to the R (a narrow side path where you must exercise care and keep a tight hold on children), when the weather is favourable the pointed tor of Win Hill appears, peeping up above the vast lower slopes of Thornhill Brink to the NE. In these conditions, part of the extensive edges of the Kinder plateau may also be observed, these rising impressively to the NW. There are also extensive views of the Hope Valley and of the undulating ridge from Mam Tor, leading over the crumbling face of Back Tor to Lose Hill.

Retrace your steps diligently back to the gate, go through it and continue along the main path, which then threads through higher ground where the grassy sides of the widening dale progressively decline, becoming less spectacular. The route passes through stone pillars and then flattens off as it makes its way between the petering-out sides of the dale, which is now no more than a shallow hollow in the surrounding hillsides. The footpath changes from a rough and stony way to a grassy channel, which unfortunately sometimes becomes muddy and waterlogged following prolonged rain. The flattening dale bends progressively to the R to pass through an unusual, vertically railed gate, near to which a helpful route map of the area has been posted.

The obvious way then tracks w to pass through a second iron gate positioned in recently renovated limestone walling. Walk towards the brow ahead, keeping to the line of the adjacent stone wall to your R and ignoring the cart track which rises further L. Now use a wide grassy path which bears L, climbing slightly uphill and following the changing direction of the wall as it continues ssw towards the hillock and quarry workings visible ahead to your L. You will reach and go through a wooden gate, and then cross over a stepped w-stile next to a second gate, where you will find an intersection of ways at MR 135813.

Turn R to cross over another w-stile and begin walking w along a wide, enclosed track. The next section of the route leads for about 1km (¾ mile) across flattish, grassy uplands, these divided into sheep pastures by numerous limestone walls. From here, the rolling hillsides of Old Moor to your L lead S, dropping towards the village of Peak Forest. Cross over a W-stile as you continue W and ignore a wide track which leads off R towards Mam Tor as the obvious way leads up the shallow rise ahead, passing through disused gate posts. However, turn off full R when you approach the next gate, to continue NNW up rising ground beside another limestone wall on your L.

The route then threads through undulating, excavated slopes by means of a narrow path comprised of stones and compacted soil, which in places is not very clearly defined. The way continues N passing over the crest of the brow at the highest point of the entire route, near to the disused Slitherstone Mine. The views ahead, which include part of the Kinder plateau, Mam Tor, Lose Hill and the tip of Win Hill, should be familiar to you. Descend directly in line with far-away Mam Tor, still walking N to cross a stone wall which bars your way by means of a stile. The grassy path continues down across expansive, open slopes and then bears L down a slightly steeper gradient. You will pass the buildings of Oxlow Farm some distance away to your L and your path then converges with a narrow lane at MR 127826.

Turn R along the road and follow it as it bends sharply L, disregarding the turning off leading E towards the Winnats Pass.

The limestone gorge of the Winnats Pass.

However, a short distance further on you should escape over a w-stile on the R, near to which is a sign for 'Winnats Head Farm'. A waymarked footpath leads E from here over another stile to skirt the boundary walling of the farm to your R, which you have veered to the R to reach. Keeping to the path signed 'To Winnats Pass', cross a farm track and continue down the path adjacent to the road and separated from it by a stone wall. Disregard ways off and stiles providing access to them, to continue beside the road into and through the spectacular limestone gorge, where examples of fossils may be spotted on the pearly white, limestone cliff faces. Cross over a w-stile, and then as you continue downwards there will not be much for you to think about apart from the sensational scenery surrounding you.

You will then pass the entrance to Speedwell Cavern, with its well-stocked gift shop. If you have time, a boat trip to the end of the cave is well worthwhile. Within 50 paces of passing the shop, turn R over the w-stile to continue along the path which leads further E through the High Peak Estate of Longcliff (owned by the National Trust). The obvious way threads along the R flank of the Hope Valley, through a G-stile and then along stretches which become muddy in wet weather, into the outskirts of Castleton. The path continues more steeply downhill along an enclosed section, to connect with a surfaced lane ahead. A visit to Peak Cavern is an option, and to reach the entrance to this you should turn R along the private road (also a footpath) and then R again to reach the massive opening positioned at the bottom of awesome, vertical rock faces.

Afterwards, walk back down towards the centre of Castleton, this time bearing R to follow the course of the stream. Then turn R again to cross the arched stone bridge and bear L along the narrow lane beside the stream, following this enclosed way down to the main road ahead, which is reached directly opposite the entrance to the carpark.

TACKLING THE WALK

CASUAL WALKERS

This route should find favour with casual walkers: there is plenty of exercise involved, although this is never too strenuous, and features of interest all along the way.

FAMILY WALKERS

Families with young children will probably not get too far up Cave Dale – not necessarily because of the climbing involved, but rather due to the unfair competition from the many other attractions in and around Castleton.

STRONG, EXPERIENCED WALKERS

This walk is very suitable for strong walkers, who will probably want to extend it to include Mam Tor and Lose Hill.

PLACES OF INTEREST

CASTLETON

Situated at the w end of the Hope Valley, Castleton is one of the major tourist attractions of the Peak District. It is well endowed with hotels, inns, guest houses, cafés and gift shops, and there are many fascinating attractions nearby including Cave Dale, Peveril Castle, Peak Cavern, Speedwell Cavern, the Winnats Pass, Treak Cliff Cavern and the Blue John Cavern and Mine. The village is promoted as 'the gem of the Peaks' due to its association with the semi-precious mineral Blue John, which is mined in the area and nowhere else in the world.

PEVERIL CASTLE

The ruins of Peveril Castle rise high on a craggy ridge above Castleton. William Peveril, one of William the Conqueror's most trusted knights, built his fortifications on this almost impregnable site with its commanding views across the Hope Valley.

PEAK CAVERN

Peak Cavern is situated beneath the remains of Peveril Castle in a vertical cliff face. The entrance to the cave is the largest of any in Europe. The half-hour tour of the cavern starts along a low passage known as 'Lumbago Walk' and this leads to the Great Cave – at 28m (90ft) long by 46m (150ft) wide, the largest cavity open to the public in Great Britain. Further attractions include an underground waterfall and an Orchestral Chamber where choirs used to entertain visitors in perfect acoustic surroundings.

SPEEDWELL CAVERN

This cavern is located at the foot of the Winnats Pass, to the w of Castleton. Reaching the cavern involves a climb down 105 steps to board a boat, which will transport you along an underground canal through the workings of a 200-year-old lead mine. The spectacular cavern at the end of this incredible journey contains the awesome Bottomless Pit – a huge subterranean lake. There is a well-stocked gift shop at the entrance to the cavern, where jewellery made from the world-famous Blue John stone may be purchased. Light refreshments are also available here.

BLUE JOHN CAVERN AND MINE AND TREAK CLIFF CAVERN

See Walk 4, page 41.

13 MILLER'S DALE, CHEE DALE AND WORMHILL

**STARTING/
FINISHING POINT**
Miller's Dale carpark
OLM 24: MR 138733

**GRADING
OF WALK**
Easy/straight-
forward

**TIME
ALLOWANCE**
3 hours

DISTANCE
7.6km (4.7 miles)

**TOTAL HEIGHT
GAINED**
150m (490ft)

HIGHEST POINT
Near Wormhill
315m (1035ft)

GRADIENTS

Stiff climb out of Chee Dale, but this is soon over. Further on, the descent back into the dale is not so steep.

PARKING

Large, surfaced carpark at the former railway station.

PUBLIC TRANSPORT

Bus routes 65, 66, 181, 202, 309 and 795.

OVERVIEW/INTEREST

Spectacular, limestone gorge of Chee Dale with adventurous stepping stones. Magnificent views throughout the walk. Plenty of wildlife and varied flora, including wild orchids. Village of Wormhill with ancient stocks.

AMENITIES

Toilets and a picnic area at the carpark, plus a mobile Peak National Park Information Centre. Refreshments available at the café in Wormhill.

FOOTPATHS AND WAYSIGNS

Paths vary between not so good, average, good and very good. Some waterlogged areas, but few of any significance. Route finding relatively straightforward, with adequate signs along the way, particularly on the Monsal Trail.

F ROM the parking area, pass through the wrought-iron gate and follow the wide path signed 'Monsal Trail', passing by the remaining buildings of the disused railway station on your R. Walk parallel to the former platforms, following the way now signed 'Monsal Trail, Chee Dale, Buxton', bearing R to do this. Ignore a side path leading off to the L and continue heading W along the level pathway. Turn off L along a narrower path, passing by another sign reading 'Monsal Trail, Miller's Dale' and a plaque detailing some of the extensive flora to be observed along the trail.

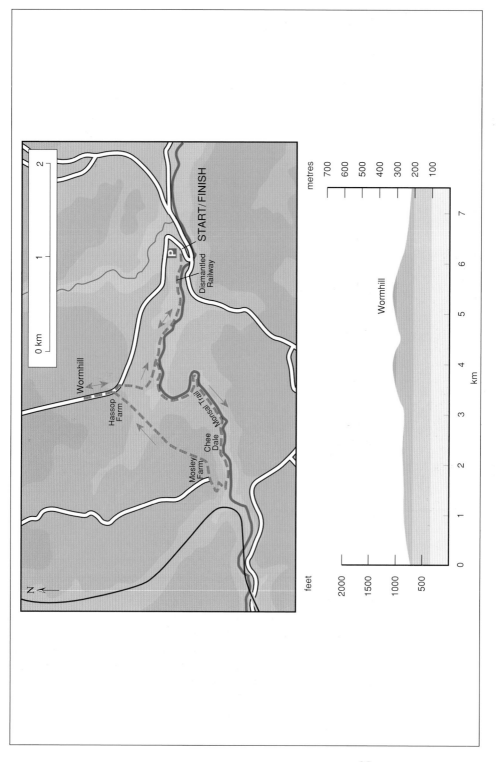

*Stepping stones
in use in Chee
Dale.*

101

The way descends steps to reach the River Wye flowing sedately below between wooded banks. Turn sharp R before reaching the road to pass through a gap in the stone wall, and then turn R again to walk NW along Chee Dale beside the river. The wide, obvious path, recently refurbished in places, leads W close to the meandering stream through the steep-sided, wooded dale past outcrops of carboniferous limestone. The mature trees are predominantly sycamore, with some beech further on, and beneath their spreading boughs a multitude of wild flowers thrive including pink campion, ramsons, forget-me-nots and butterbur, these all spotted in one tiny area.

The continuation way passes beneath an impressively high stone bridge, now also redundant. Immediately after passing beneath this arch, ignore a stepped way signed 'Monsal Trail' leading up to the R. The path then narrows as you proceed further upstream, and further on you must ignore a railed, metalled bridge spanning the river to continue in the direction again signed 'Chee Dale'. The dale then widens considerably as the River Wye tumbles down over a succession of low and irregular stone weirs. The dale then narrows once more and you will have to negotiate a

The perpendicular limestone cliffs of Chee Dale.

craggy protrusion of exposed rock. After this you will cross a plank bridge spanning a tributary watercourse; near here, ignore a path leading up out of the dale to Wormhill, instead bearing L over the w-stile and across another plank.

The continuation path then leads uphill, backtracking for a short distance before curving to lead further sw along and above the meandering river to your L. The slippery, sometimes muddy, path then threads over limestone crags back down to the bed of the river – take particular care on this short descent. There is often more mud underfoot as you pass by a spectacular vertical cliff face on the far side of the river. The way then leads for some distance beneath a rock overhang which is favoured by climbers. Watch out for the drips of water which constantly percolate through the porous limestone above! Towards the end of the overhang, the way upstream is across partly submerged stepping stones, which disappear below the surface of the water when the river is in spate – be extremely careful crossing these in such conditions.

Cross over the river via the railed wooden footbridge, which is positioned near to another impressive arched bridge from the disused railway line that you pass beneath immediately after turning R along the waymarked continuation footpath. From here a stepped way leads further upstream; continue ahead along Chee Dale, ignoring a signed concession path traversing to the L and signed 'To trail'. A short distance further on, re-cross the river over another wooden bridge. A sign now alerts you to the nature reserve and requests you to avoid doing damage or disturbing the wildlife.

You will now pass more limestone overhangs, complete with climbers' slings and hooks, followed by an area of scree poised menacingly on the steep slopes to your R. High limestone cliffs then appear ahead, providing even more spectacular scenery, and you will then need to negotiate a second, less demanding section of stepping stones below another limestone overhang. The narrow way continues to thread over craggy ground, now heading towards a really dominating, vertical limestone cliff positioned on the far side of the river. Yet another disused railway arch then throws a shadow across your path as you ignore steps leading off to the R and cross over a wooden stile ahead.

Just before reaching a gap in a stone wall, and as another viaduct comes into view, veer R along a narrow diagonal path which leads initially through nettles on an upward traverse out of the dale. Bear R again further up to continue climbing the hillside, now keeping to a wide grassy path. Further on, the obvious way zigzags up the steepish, grassy slope; towards the top of the hill, ignore a grassy way which leads through a gap in a wall on your L. Eventually the upward slope levels off, and a short distance further on you should climb over a W-stile to the L of a metal gate. Turn R along the route signed 'Public bridleway' to head ENE past Mosley Farm, where it can be muddy. The way upgrades to a farm lane signed to 'Wormhill' as you ignore the turning to the L.

Cross over the cattle grid at Alsop Farm, after which the walled lane swings sharply to the L. Ignore a W-stile on your R as you continue N along the flat, surfaced lane. However, a short distance further on you should turn off R along the signed public footpath, which is accessed through a wooden gate and W-stile. Walk diagonally across the adjacent field, now heading NE towards the farm buildings across the valley. Keep to this direction, crossing more meadows and passing through broken-down stone walling (using a waysigned G-stile to cross one of these). The route then zigzags downhill and crosses the deep-sided grassy valley of Flag Dale, where you cross over another W-stile, disregarding a path leading off at right angles to the L. Wild orchids bloom in this area and their purple spikes blanket the grassy slopes in late May.

Climb out of the dale, keeping to the stony path, which reverts to grass at the top to lead through a G-stile in a stone wall ahead. After this, the grassy path tracks further NE towards Wormhill, passing through another G-stile to reach the cluster of buildings that signifies you have reached Hassop Farm, at MR 123739. Pass through two gated G-stiles and bear R between the farm buildings to reach the road ahead. There is now an optional detour to visit Wormhill and perhaps also sample the refreshments available at the Farmhouse Tea Room situated in the village (where boots are welcome provided your feet are in them!). To do this, turn L and follow the road the short distance into the attractive village.

Afterwards, retrace your steps back to where you first came out on to the road near Hassop Farm and continue on past. (Should you not wish to go to Wormhill, simply turn R when you first reach this point.) Walk downhill along the road, following it as it curves to the L, but then turn off along the public footpath signed 'Chee Dale ½ and Blackwell', immediately passing a bungalow named Chee-Tor Cottage. From here a secluded walled path leads gently downhill beneath trees, passing between redundant stone pillars. Disregard the branch path leading more steeply down on your R and keep to the higher ground by walking along the continuation path, which then bends L along fairly level land above Chee Dale.

A narrow but clearly defined path then tracks ESE parallel to the meandering River Wye, far below at the bottom of the densely wooded dale. The path then leads gradually down to the floor of the dale, crossing a section of terraced rocks in the process. The descent brings you into Chee Dale opposite the railed footbridge which you passed earlier in the day, when walking up the dale. Turn L to retrace your outward steps along the dale as far as the first viaduct. This time, branch off up the stone steps just before the bridge, following the waysigned 'Monsal Trail'. Crinoid fossils may be inspected in the paving slabs towards the top of these steps.

Turn L along the Monsal Trail: this was originally a Manchester to London main-line passenger route operated by Midland Railway. You will immediately pass some interesting disused lime kilns on your L, instantly recognized by the massive concrete buttresses added in the 1920s. These kilns were worked until 1944. From here, follow the virtually flat trail along a relatively short distance back to the carpark.

TACKLING THE WALK

CASUAL WALKERS
This is a splendid and rewarding circuit and should be enjoyed by most walkers. Be careful not to arrange the walk when the River Wye is in flood, as you might then have to cross submerged, slippery stepping stones.

FAMILY WALKERS
The walk should also appeal to families with older children, but is not suitable for those with tiny tots due to the stepping stones and other awkward passages. Such groups are advised to keep to the area around the Miller's Dale carpark, venturing for short distances along that dale and Chee Dale.

STRONG, EXPERIENCED WALKERS
For strong walkers, this short route may be extended by walking further w into Wye Dale and/or progressing further E into Miller's Dale.

PLACES OF INTEREST

WORMHILL
Wormhill is more a small cluster of buildings than a village. These comprise farms, a café and St Margaret's Church with its Saxon tower. The centre of activity is a grassy dell which contains a well – dressed each year – stocks and a splendid stone memorial to James Brindley, the famous civil engineer who was born in the parish at nearby Tunstead in 1716.

14 TIDESWELL DALE, MILLER'S DALE, CRESSBROOK, CRESSBROOK DALE AND TANSLEY DALE

**STARTING/
FINISHING POINT**
Tideswell Dale
carpark OLM 24:
MR 154742

**GRADING
OF WALK**
Moderate/
challenging (just!)

**TIME
ALLOWANCE**
3 hours

DISTANCE
8.2km (5.1 miles)

**TOTAL HEIGHT
GAINED**
160m (525ft)

HIGHEST POINT
Above Tansley Dale
300m (985ft)

GRADIENTS
No sustained, severe climbing. Ascents and descents are well spaced out.

PARKING
Large carpark holds up to 40 cars.

PUBLIC TRANSPORT
Bus routes 65, 67, X67, 173, 181, 202, 400, 460 and 795.

OVERVIEW/INTEREST
Walk through several spectacular, interconnected limestone dales. Magnificent scenery throughout. Features include Litton Mill, Water-cum-Jolly and Cressbrook. Plenty of wildlife.

AMENITIES
Toilets and a picnic area at the carpark. Refreshments available *en route* at Litton Mill and near Cressbrook Mill.

FOOTPATHS AND WAYSIGNS
Paths are good to excellent for most of way. Some narrow paths where route finding is challenging. Ground is well drained and usually firm underfoot.

DEPART from the lower end of the carpark, walking past the information point to enter Tideswell Dale and heading s along a wide, well-surfaced path. The upper section of the dale contains a mixture of deciduous trees including beech, elderberry, hawthorn, hazel, sycamore and willow. Disregard a side track heading uphill on the L signed 'Picnic area and trail', and keep to the dale bottom as steeper, wooded slopes rise above. Further on, keep L when the paths divide, although these do reconnect further down the valley. Limestone cliff faces now appear as the valley curves around to the R and you will cross the tiny watercourse via a wooden footbridge.

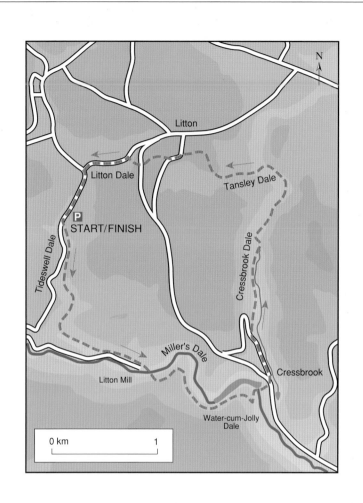

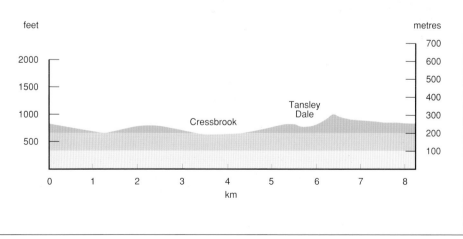

Don't talk about letting grass grow beneath your feet at Litton Mill!

Continue down the meandering dale as more limestone outcrops loom up above to your R and the ground cover thickens up, with wild flowers competing for space among the more pervasive thistles and nettles. The dale then narrows and you will cross another footbridge, where those wearing shorts will do well to avoid being stung by the nettles. After passing through an enclosed area next to an arresting limestone cliff face, the path connects with a surfaced lane at MR 157731. Turn L along this to walk E along Miller's Dale, initially through another wooded area where the River Wye comes into view on your R. You will then reach the cluster of buildings at Litton Mill, where Litton Mill Pottery enterprisingly provides refreshments and bed and breakfast may be obtained at the Barn House. Altogether, this is a most delightful spot.

Go through a gap in the stone wall on your R to access the continuation footpath waysigned 'Trail 200yd: Taddington 1½ miles' (this important turning is almost opposite the tea shop.) Cross the River Wye, where there is a delightful view back towards Litton Mill set in its tranquil location screened by surrounding trees. Climb up the railed steps on the far side and follow the zigzags of the path leading up and above the steep-sided dale. When you reach the wide Monsal Trail turn sharp L along it, taking the sign 'No through way 250yd ahead' with a pinch of salt!

Your changed direction is E along the disused railway line and you can make rapid progress along this flat trail to arrive at the blocked-off tunnel entrance ahead. Before reaching this barrier, veer L along the narrow path, misleadingly signed 'No access' to reach an s-stile and dog gate – these features must be intended for use by walkers! There are superb views both up and down Miller's Dale from just above the blocked-off tunnel entrance. Continue with care along the narrow path, which traverses the rounded, grassy slopes of the dale and progressively gains height. Your way then bisects another path, where you continue to track uphill along the better-defined route. From here, the views down into Miller's Dale become increasingly spectacular as high, vertical limestone cliffs plunge down into the recesses of the wooded, meandering dale.

Your gravel-surfaced path merges with another and you should bear L at this point, immediately passing a group of small caves on your R which are favoured by both sheep and walkers in inclement weather. From here, keep to the main continuation paths that contort high above the dale at a more or less constant height, ignoring all side paths and watching out for some eroded, loose ground ahead. Some distance on the main path descends temporarily, and there are two s-stiles to cross at a section of wire fencing just before the dale swings around sharply to the L. After this, the path levels out again and the angled surface underfoot becomes rougher.

Eventually, the buildings of Cressbrook appear on the far side of the dale, with Water-cum-Jolly located at the base of the near-vertical limestone cliffs below, at the bottom of the valley. You will now have to negotiate more sections of loose scree with care, before rounding another prolonged grassy brow. Beyond these expansive slopes, the path gradually descends into the valley along a fairly straight traverse. Your approach connects with a wider path below, along which you turn sharp L to continue down towards the rather stark industrial buildings of Cressbrook, following a path now surfaced with gravel and loose stones. The descent funnels into a zigzag flight of stone steps and you will re-cross the River Wye at the bottom using a substantial wooden footbridge positioned just below a weir.

The weir holds back the water to form a delightful pool, and a short detour around to the L and across a wooden footbridge will enable you to admire the splendid views from this quiet spot. Afterwards, continue past the building materials compound, where you will come to the unusual Brew Stop – where drinks may be purchased but you are allowed to eat your own food. After this, walk around the extensive refurbishments being carried out at Cressbrook Mill to reach the road ahead. Turn L, signed to 'Cressbrook: Litton 2', to walk N uphill beneath trees. You now enter Cressbrook Dale, sometimes referred to as Raven Dale (or Ravensdale) due to the associated bird life, although ravens were banished from the White Peak in the last century. The dale winds below you as a steep-sided, densely wooded valley.

Keep walking uphill, disregarding a track off to the L, until you approach a hairpin bend. Before you reach this, bear R along a surfaced side lane signed 'Ravensdale: no through road'. Superb views then open up through the intervening foliage on your R of the perpendicular limestone cliffs rearing high above from the densely wooded slopes below. These formidable crags are only for birds and very experienced climbers! Keep to the surfaced lane to pass a row of delightfully situated stone cottages, their tiny gardens brimming with brightly coloured flowers in season. Beyond these, continue along the signed public footpath towards Wardlow. This leads through overgrown foliage, where in summer flies can be a nuisance.

Cross the stream via a footbridge, where a sign welcomes you to the nature reserve of Cressbrook Dale. A second sign warns you about dangerous mine shafts and advises you to keep to the designated footpaths. Ahead, fork L along the lower footpath, keeping to the bottom of the dale where you will walk through a wooded area. The path emerges from the trees to penetrate the more open upper reaches of the dale. An obvious path continues to wind up the valley, and further on a traverse path descends from the R to merge with yours. The combined path then leads beside the bed of the stream, where unfortunately the surrounding land often becomes boggy after prolonged rain.

The route then leads to the confluence with Tansley Dale to the W, as Cressbrook Dale meanders further N. Use the waysigned P-stile on your L to walk into Tansley Dale along a grassy path. This dry dale rises gradually, narrowing as it goes, to lead through limestone outcrops and into more rounded grassy slopes above. The ground then levels off following a final upwards diagonal to your R, which terminates at another P-stile. Climb over this, and keep to the faint grassy path as it bears R away from the stile. The continuation way skirts the corner of a dry stone wall as it leads towards two metal gates ahead. Climb over the W-stile between these gates and then turn L along the wide, walled track which leads W. Avoid all side paths, to reach the surfaced road a short distance further on at MR 165749. Bear slightly L along this, heading away from the village of Litton.

When the lane bends sharply to the L, select the signed public footpath straight ahead, accessing this through a narrow G-stile. Continue along the edge of the adjacent field beside stone walling on your R. Cross the W-stile ahead and walk along the side of the next meadow, where the buildings of Litton may be spotted to

110

your R. This pattern continues as you cross two more w-stiles, the second of these a squeezer (a narrow G-stile). The way then bends diagonally L to reach another lane which you should cross over. A stile provides access to the continuation of the path, which then descends steeply into Litton Dale, where you will reach the road opposite Dale House.

Go through the G-stile, turn L along the footpath adjacent to the road and follow this in the direction of Tideswell. The path and road lead down to a T-junction at the major B6049 road below. Turn L here, to walk away from Tideswell. Within 20 paces, use the stile on your L to access the footpath and follow this safe, grassy way adjacent to the busy road s down the valley. Walk along the faint path as it passes through small copses of trees, always keeping to the lower ground nearest to the road. The path leads over a stile and passes under a line of mature beech trees to re-enter the carpark.

TACKLING THE WALK

CASUAL WALKERS
This route should appeal to casual walkers, although if you do not relish heights you should short-circuit the high-level section above Miller's Dale by walking straight along the bottom of the valley.

FAMILY WALKERS
Similar remarks apply to family groups, except that those with young children should definitely keep to the Monsal Trail along Miller's Dale, thus avoiding any exposure high above.

STRONG, EXPERIENCED WALKERS
This is an interesting short walk with some mild exposure, which should make an enjoyable half-day excursion for more experienced walkers of all levels of competence.

PLACES OF INTEREST

LITTON MILL AND CRESSBROOK MILL
These mills are relics from a bygone industrial age when workers, including young children and orphans, had to toil long hours tending the looms for a mere pittance, disgracefully exploited in harsh working conditions. Cressbrook Mill was actually something of an exception to this unfortunate norm, in that Richard Arkwright was far more humane in operating this cotton mill and his apprentices even received an elementary education.

111

15 ASHFORD IN THE WATER, MONSAL HEAD AND MONSAL DALE

**STARTING/
FINISHING POINT**
Carpark at Ashford
OLM 24: MR 195698

**GRADING
OF WALK**
Moderate/
challenging

**TIME
ALLOWANCE**
3½ hours

DISTANCE
8.9km (5.5 miles)

**TOTAL HEIGHT
GAINED**
230m (755ft)

HIGHEST POINT
Towards Monsal
Head 265m (870ft)

GRADIENTS
Some gradual climbs of varying steepness, with a steep descent into Monsal Dale.

PARKING
Tiny walled carpark holds up to 15 cars.

PUBLIC TRANSPORT
Bus services 58, 68, 153, 173, 202, R1 and X23.

OVERVIEW/INTEREST
Fairytale setting of Ashford in the Water. Admire the grandeur of Monsal Head and Monsal Dale. Spectacular limestone scenery throughout, with superb distant views. Abundant wild life: animals, birds and fish.

AMENITIES
Toilets at the carpark and at Monsal Head, where refreshments are also available. Ashford has several hotels, inns and guest houses offering refreshments. Picnic site at the carpark at Lees Bottom, just off the A6(T) road.

FOOTPATHS AND WAYSIGNS
Paths are nearly all good to excellent. Occasional sections of rougher ground with odd wet spots. Signs are adequate throughout.

TURN L from the carpark and walk W along Court Lane to reach the road and grassy island ahead. You will pass Corner Cottage, an attractive bed and breakfast establishment, on your L to get there. Turn R to walk uphill along Vicarage Lane, but within 50 paces cross over and turn off up the path signed 'Monsal Dale 2'. This initially tracks back acutely on your line of approach, leading uphill beneath foliage. However, the path almost immediately turns R to continue up a stepped way, where geese, goats and sheep graze the small enclosed fields on your L. Pass through a G-stile in a stone wall, and beyond this a second such stile will provide

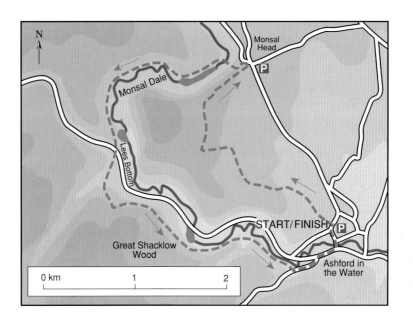

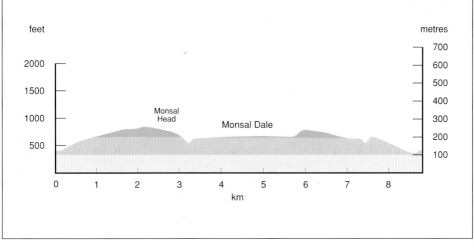

113

access to more open countryside. The continuation way is signed to 'Monsal Head'.

The ridge of Longstone Edge now appears over to your R in the NNE. With this in sight, walk directly across the adjacent field, heading NNW towards the brow ahead. Then veer slightly L and NW to walk towards the R corner of the field, crossing over the stepped W-stile positioned a few paces from this corner. Turn L along the walled lane on the far side. The obvious continuation way then winds gently uphill heading WNW, to pass the attractive bungalow named Ploverfield, at MR 189702½. The way, a walled lane leading through expansive landscapes of orderly pastures and low limestone hillsides, gradually climbs further uphill and then bends decisively to the R at three gates to pass a cattle dew pond on your L.

From here, the enclosed track leads predominantly northwards, where it terminates at a rusty gate and S-stile. Use this stile to follow the continuation path, again helpfully signed to 'Monsal Head' at this point. This is on the L, adjacent to a crumbling dry stone wall. The grassy way now leads W, gaining marginal additional height. Cross over another W-stile, next to a metal gate, and then immediately turn full R (at MR 180706), as directed, to continue N towards Monsal Head, avoiding private land above on your L. A further G-stile then provides entry to another walled track. From here, the waysigned route leads further N, negotiating more stiles and gates along the way. Soon the first views of the spectacular limestone scenery surrounding Monsal Head will appear, and these just get better and better, revealing progressively more of the steep-sided dale as you approach. Far away up the dale, the huddle of buildings forming Cressbrook may be identified to the NNW.

The path leads gently down to the hustle and bustle of Monsal Head, always a busy place. The approach is down steps and the final hurdle is a wooden S-stile. Along here, be aware of the steep fall-away on your L and hold tightly on to young children. The views along meandering Monsal Dale from the edge of the smaller of the two parking areas are supreme, and seats are provided here for you to drool over these in relative comfort. Leave this splendid viewing spot across the minor road which links with Cressbrook, but immediately turn off through a gap in the stone walling on the far side. Turn R to descend the steps leading to the viaduct below, along the route signed 'Monsal Dale: viaduct and trail'.

The path leads fairly steeply downhill and you should turn sharp L to continue heading towards the viaduct and trail. You will reach the disused railway below near to the sealed-off tunnel entrance. Turn R and cross the viaduct, which provides breathtaking views for those who have a head for heights. Otherwise, just concentrate on walking across! Turn sharp L through the swing gate at the far end of the high bridge. Then bear L, and L again, to complete the descent into the tranquil wooded valley of Monsal Dale. The final drop down is relatively steep and the eroded path does become slippery when wet.

Bear R along the bottom of the dale to walk W on the obvious, worn footpath, heading downstream in company with abundant, noisy waterfowl. The next 2.5km (1½ miles) of the walk are along the narrowing dale, past limestone cliffs, an attractive weir and never far away from the meandering River Wye. Ignore all side paths leading away from the floor of the dale or crossing the river as you progress down the wooded valley, to connect with the main A6(T) road at Lees Bottom (MR 171706). Cross a muddy brook just before you reach the road and access this busy artery by climbing up the steps and passing through a G-stile. Cross the road with care, selecting a diagonal to your L, and then bear further L and then R to reach the stepped path leading above the White Lodge carparking area.

The disused railway viaduct at Monsal Head.

The River Wye makes a tempting place for a paddle.

Climb over the s-stile and follow the wide path signed as part of local walks 2 and 3. Cross over a second similar stile, to follow the way as it curves R up into the densely wooded valley, which narrows progressively. Then avoid the path leading local walk 2 uphill to your R by following the continuation of walk 3 along the level traverse to the L. Your immediate surroundings now become more enclosed and craggy, with areas of exposed limestone bedrock accompanying your progress uphill. A short distance further on, be particularly careful to turn L over the stile to keep company with walk 3 (the rocky way directly ahead leads towards Deep Dale). You will need to negotiate a narrow, rocky funnel before the dale opens out again, where your path climbs more steeply up a widening grassy valley lined with hawthorn trees.

Keep to the obvious, narrow stony path which zigzags up the hillsides ahead, leading you to a footpath sign which reads '3 footpath: Ashford/Sheldon'. Turn L here, in the opposite direction to another path leading to Deep Dale. More steady climbing follows along a diagonal traverse which leads into more woodland, mainly of hawthorn and beech. Use a wide wooden stile to cross a dry stone wall; walk 3 does likewise. The path then bears L up a small section of rock before quickly levelling off again to round the brow of the hillside. There are some steep drops to your L along here, so keep a tight hold on young children. An obvious way continues to wind through the trees at the edge of Great Shacklow Wood between SE and E, heading back towards Ashford, now some 2.5km (1½ miles) away.

You will gradually lose height as you progress along the clear path through the woodland, where you pass through a particularly delightful glade of sycamore. The way emerges from the main woodland and another path is intersected at right angles: do not turn off along it. Instead, continue walking SE, where you may disturb pheasants. You will pass an attractive tree-fringed pool, and beyond this a wider, flatter path tracks closer to the River Wye to lead you past a disused water mill. Rather unusually, this has rusting water wheels on either side. Further on, disregard the bridge across the river to continue tracking along the valley. You will pass through a number of stile-and-gate combinations before the path connects with a surfaced lane at MR 189694.

Turn L down the lane to reach the A6(T) road again, making maximum use of the pavement on the near side before crossing carefully near Sheepwash Bridge, well away from the bends. Then cross the River Wye again via this attractive arched stone bridge. Pass by the rounded former market stall, bear slightly L along Fennel Street and the carpark is then a short distance further on to the R.

TACKLING THE WALK

CASUAL WALKERS
A really fine walk full of interest, which is ideal for walkers seeking half a day or so of not too strenuous exercise.

FAMILY WALKERS
This route is also suitable for families with older children, but there are some relatively steep drops and other ups and downs to contend with along the way which render the walk too exacting for smaller ones. The advice here is to use the car to travel the short distance between Ashford and Monsal Head, and then spend your time exploring the immediate surroundings of these two places of interest (see below).

STRONG, EXPERIENCED WALKERS
A walk that may easily be extended to encompass the Longstone villages to the N and/or Deep Dale and Sheldon to the S.

PLACES OF INTEREST

ASHFORD IN THE WATER
This is a delightful village occupying a fairytale setting. In addition to the amenities detailed on page 112, it has many other interesting attractions including Sheepwash Bridge, a medieval pack-horse crossing of the River Wye sited near the original ford, and the Church of the Holy Trinity, originally Norman but rebuilt in 1870. The village grew up around the ford on an ancient trading route known as The Portway, and it remained a centre for the thriving local leadmining industry until the late nineteenth century.

MONSAL HEAD AND VIADUCT
The limestone features of Monsal Dale must rank among the very best to be found anywhere in the White Peak. These come to perfection at Monsal Head, where the River Wye flows through a flat, meandering valley lined with vertical cliffs of awesome proportions. This superb scenery results largely from water carving a course through a dome of carboniferous limestone, layered some 300 million years ago when the region was covered by a warm, shallow sea.

The Midland Railway line from Manchester to London passed through the dale between 1867 and 1968, and the railway viaduct at Monsal Head is now listed as being of 'architectural and historic interest'. It has not always been that way, and among many other critics the philosopher John Ruskin expressed strong feelings about this monstrosity which despoiled beautiful countryside.

16 BASLOW AND CHATSWORTH HOUSE AND PARK

GRADIENTS

Nothing of real significance. One short and easy climb from Chatsworth Park to woodland above and then back to the lower ground.

PARKING

Large carpark near the centre of the town.

PUBLIC TRANSPORT

Principal town with extensive bus services, both local and long distance.

OVERVIEW/INTEREST

Starts from the attractive town of Baslow, with Bar Brook and thatched cottages. Features stately Chatsworth House with its majestic gardens and parkland. Includes sections through deciduous woodlands and around Emperor Lake. Extensive flora and fauna. Great appeal for children.

AMENITIES

Toilet at the carpark. Baslow is crammed with hotels, inns, restaurants, cafés and a sweet shop. More toilets and high-quality refreshment facilities at Chatsworth House.

FOOTPATHS AND WAYSIGNS

Paths are very good and clear for most of the route, with virtually no boggy ground. Exception is around the lake where paths are narrower and less well defined, and there are some wet patches after heavy rain.

TURN R out of the carpark and walk past Sweet Gene's Olde Worlde Confectionery Shop, with its assortment of toffees from a sadly bygone era! Use the attractive stone hump-backed bridge to cross Bar Brook and then turn immediately R along the footpath signed to 'Chatsworth' to pass by a row of rustic thatched cottages (these are particularly photogenic). Pass through the wrought-iron G-stile and continue SW down the enclosed lane, following this around to the L and ignoring a K-gate and path leading off to the R. A short distance further on, enter Chatsworth Park through an imposing gate set into a high, stone wall.

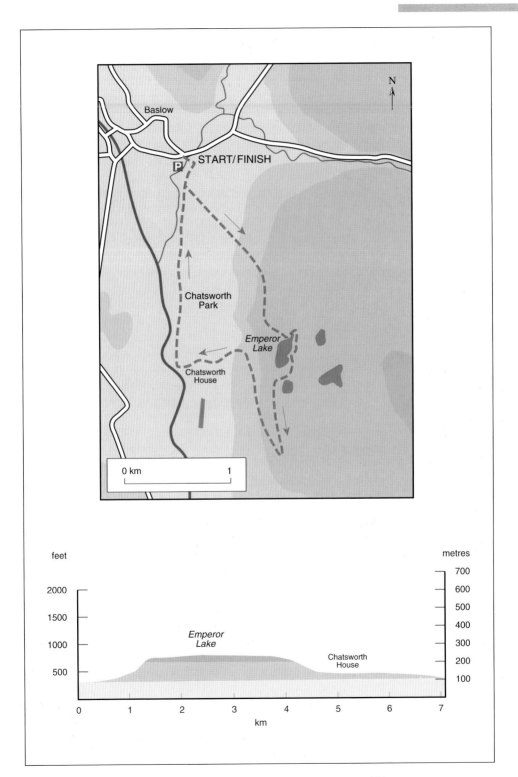

Veer immediately half L to follow the direction across the flat parkland indicated by a sign reading 'Concession footpath: Stand Tower 1 mile: Beeley 3½ miles'. Your changed bearing is SE across the immaculately maintained parklands of Chatsworth, which contain many fine specimen trees including mature beech, cherry, chestnut, oak and sycamore. The way crosses one of the entrance drives on a diagonal as you walk towards the tree-covered edge ahead. Along here you will catch the first glimpses of Chatsworth House away to the SSW over to your R. Keep tracking SE, making for a gap in the trees directly ahead, to bisect another estate track as the ground ahead rises very gently. Then skirt to the L of a sparse group of trees and head up the grassy slope ahead. You will cross or temporarily walk along further internal gravel tracks during your diagonal SE approach to the wooded escarpment directly ahead. Trim your final approach to this, to reach a wooden bench positioned near to a caged sapling oak tree.

The views from this memorial seat back across the lush parkland to the expansive, tree-speckled green hillsides beyond are both spectacular and peaceful. When you have rested, climb over the s-stile positioned in the stone boundary wall above to enter the trees. From here a wide, clearly defined path leads uphill along a diagonal to the R through mixed woodland, to reach the edge above. May is one of the best months in which to walk this way, for then the ground is covered in a carpet of bluebells.

At the top of the edge, bear r along the wide path surfaced with chippings, signed 'Concession footpath: Stand Tower: Beeley 2½'. This is at MR 266709 and your new direction is s. Less than 0.5km (¼ mile) further on, make a short detour to your R to take in the magnificent views of Chatsworth House and Gardens and the village of Edensor situated on the hillside beyond, both clearly visible from the grassy banks in front of the Stand Tower, a former hunting lodge. In doing this, respect that this unusual turreted building is now a private residence. Walk back to the main pathway by bearing R along a wide avenue of rhododendron. Turn R down the estate road and continue s through the attractive woodland lining the edge.

Further on fork L, following the direction indicated by an unusual purple arrow painted on a large stone. The continuation way curves L from here to lead you to the northernmost tip of Emperor Lake, a quite delightful spot. Be vigilant now to locate and turn R along a narrow path commencing just past the inlet and leading beneath trees around the E side of the lake. The next section of the walk is really delightful. As you amble along, searching out the less-well-defined continuation way, the most superb views across the lake appear continuously through gaps in the nearby foliage and the silence is broken only by the chirping of birds and their

frequent landings and take-offs from the still surface of the water. As you proceed s along here, keep to the network of paths nearest to the edge of the water, disregarding all routes on your L leading into the thickets and denser undergrowth. The only excitement along this stretch is the crossing of one particularly wide drainage ditch!

The thatched cottages near Bar Brook receive tender, loving care.

When you reach the s end of the lake track around to your R where you will be rewarded with more spectacular views across the water and its wildlife. Walk between the two boulders positioned to prevent unwelcome vehicular access, and then just before reaching the tiny stone jetty branch off L along the wide gravel path. This link will return you to the main N–S way along the edge above Chatsworth Park. Turn L along the main avenue, but within a few paces take a few strides to your R to admire the views from a position directly above the ornamental water cascades which tumble down through the formal gardens below.

Continue s through the extensive woodland, still on the level and for some distance beneath an avenue of beech trees. The way then descends very gradually as it leads further s, to connect with another internal road through the estate. Turn R here, as indicated by a second purple arrow, and walk downhill, immediately negotiating a hairpin bend to the L. Near to a bench, turn off the surfaced road by selecting a narrow path on the R. This continues to lead downhill beneath trees, short-circuiting a second hairpin

123

bend in the adjacent roadway below. The path keeps parallel to this surfaced road for some distance before it leads back to it. At the intersection veer R along the road, but within a few paces turn off L and walk down through more trees to inspect at close quarters the tall, square, perpendicular column rising ahead. However, on no account venture past the fenced-off section, and from a safe distance heed the warning 'Unsafe structure: please keep out'.

Return to the surfaced road and turn L to continue down it. Keep L when you reach another hairpin bend below, following the direction indicated by both beige and green arrows. The way leads further downhill to bring you to a position above a pond, over which there are further fine views across the parkland towards Edensor. Continue down the road, ignoring an inviting side path off to the L which is actually a cul-de-sac. A fork on the R should also be ignored. After passing through a gateway, use the gate located to the L of a cattle grid to reach the grounds surrounding the stately home of Chatsworth House, with its numerous amenities and attractions (see page 125). Some of these will almost certainly extend your visit.

A family visit to Chatsworth House!

Afterwards, walk down to Queen Mary's Bower, an elevated stone viewing square positioned just below and to the NW of Chatsworth House. From here, track N along an obvious succession of paths and ways which lead – always a short distance away

from the meandering River Derwent on your L – past a cricket ground and the private residence of White Lodge, back to the gate where you first entered Chatsworth Park. Pass through and retrace your outward steps back to the carpark.

TACKLING THE WALK

CASUAL WALKERS

This is a delightful and far from energetic short walk including much of interest, which should appeal to all walkers who like to combine sightseeing with some gentle exercise.

FAMILY WALKERS

This route is sure to be a favourite with children and families because there is something of interest for everybody. Those with tiny tots may prefer to spend their time visiting Chatsworth House and Gardens and walking through the (dead flat) parkland.

STRONG, EXPERIENCED WALKERS

This short, leisurely stroll is easily extended to take in the delights of the villages of Beeley and Edensor, and still leave plenty of time to absorb the attractions of Chatsworth.

PLACES OF INTEREST

CHATSWORTH HOUSE, GARDENS AND PARK

This much-visited stately home is a major tourist attraction and many thousands of people come here each year. It is the ancestral home of the Duke and Duchess of Devonshire but for centuries has been open to the public, the Duke and Duchess wishing to share the beauty of the house, gardens and park with its numerous visitors.

The house, with its richly decorated rooms, contains one of the finest private art collections in the world; the gardens extend to over 100 acres with rare trees and shrubs, rockeries, spectacular fountains and cascades, greenhouses and a maze; the farmyard and adventure playground will delight and test the nerve of children; and there are appetizing refreshment facilities at the Carriage House Restaurant, an information point, gift shop, farm shop and toilet facilities. Disabled visitors are well provided for, although unfortunately it is not possible for those in wheelchairs to tour the house.

The parkland and Stand Wood above extend for over 1000 acres, and there are 8km (5 miles) of footpaths and trails open to walkers. Special outdoor events are often held in these delightful and spacious surroundings.

125

17 BAKEWELL AND HADDON HALL

**STARTING/
FINISHING POINT**
Carpark at Bakewell
OLM 24: MR 221685

**GRADING
OF WALK**
Easy/straight-
forward

**TIME
ALLOWANCE**
4 hours

DISTANCE
9km (5.6 miles)

**TOTAL HEIGHT
GAINED**
235m (770ft)

HIGHEST POINT
Near Calton Pastures
285m (935ft)

GRADIENTS
Gradual and not too strenuous ascent, with a steeper way down.

PARKING
Massive, unsurfaced carpark near to the River Wye which does become soft, so park carefully.

PUBLIC TRANSPORT
Major town with numerous bus routes.

OVERVIEW/INTEREST
Starts from the market town of Bakewell. Delightful route through enclosed woodland and open landscapes. Fine, wide-ranging views towards Chatsworth Park and Beeley Moor. Explore the attractions of Haddon Hall. Return beside the meandering River Wye.

AMENITIES
No toilets at the carpark. Variety of hotels, inns, restaurants, cafés and shops in Bakewell. Further refreshment and toilet facilities in the grounds of Haddon Hall.

FOOTPATHS AND WAYSIGNS
Paths are mostly good and easy to follow, but there are some more obscure sections where route finding demands patience. Forest harvesting has caused parts of the trails to become churned up and muddy.

WALK back to the entrance to the carpark and turn R along Coombs Road. A short distance further on, turn L to follow the signed public footpath leading to 'Outrake Farm'. A surfaced lane leads uphill, heading towards the bank of wooded ground which forms the horizon. Bear R when you reach the attractive farmhouse, keeping to the continuation path signed to 'Chatsworth' by passing through an iron gate. Keep straight on when the surfaced lane bends to the L, to then gain further height

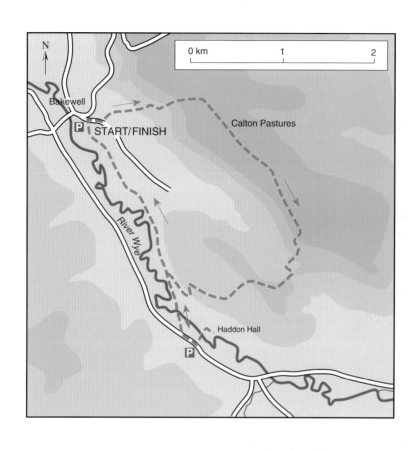

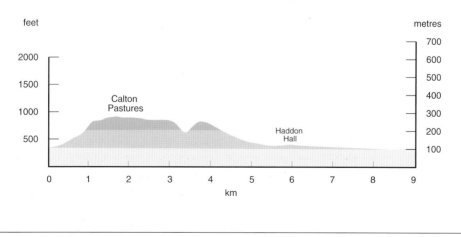

127

to the NE, walking up a grass and gravel path. Cross over the dismantled railway line, which is now part of the Monsal Trail, and continue along the obvious wide, grassy path which curves up the hillside, bisecting a golf course.

Climb over the L-stile positioned next to a metal gate and continue upwards along the waymarked path, as it curves around the rising ground to enter the deciduous woodlands. These trees are mainly beech and ash and the path weaves through them, tracking E along an easy upward gradient. Birds sing and you may disturb pheasants, as fine views appear down below to your R through gaps in the surrounding foliage. Bear R ahead along a waysigned path, to pass a notice welcoming you to Haddon Estate: 'Woodland walk: concessionary footpath: keep to waymarked path only'. When you reach the T-junction of paths ahead, turn sharp L to continue walking marginally uphill. Then, just before reaching a small brook, be careful to turn R along a narrower side path which leads more steeply uphill. You will pass a dilapidated stone building, and just beyond this the path emerges from the trees by means of an S-stile, at MR 231½688.

Out in the open once more, a grassy path – which is somewhat indistinct in places – tracks further uphill to the E to pass close to a cluster of trees on your immediate L. Bear slightly to the R along a better-defined section of path to head directly towards an S-stile above a wooden gate. Cross over this stile, which is near to a small, attractive pond ahead to your L. Instead of walking towards this, select the R path signed to 'Rowsley' to continue SE, avoiding the alternative route to your L towards Chatsworth.

The walk continues through wide, open spaces, the surrounding landscapes dotted with woodland and the higher ground leading to Beeley Moor rising in the E. Walk across the expansive fields, still tracking SE and heading towards a gate which is visible ahead. Climb over the S-stile to the L of this gate and continue along the waysigned path, from where Stand Tower (a former hunting lodge) may be spotted, rising above the trees to the NE. Further L and to the N, the buildings of Baslow and Froggatt and the gritstone edges beyond are visible in clear weather, while further L still the pointed shape of Sir William Hill with its telecommunications mast rises in the NNE.

Now bear slightly R to maintain your height and, still on a SE diagonal, head towards and just above the grassy mounds ahead, which are marked as 'Tumulus' on the OLM. A short distance further on, the path reaches the edge of the woodland at a protruding section. Walk alongside the pines and then turn R to climb over the L-stile, which provides an entry to the woods along a signed bridleway. The continuation way leads further SE from a bend to the L, which you should follow to avoid the narrow, grassy side path leading off directly ahead. The path then passes below a line of electricity cables and passes through a redundant gateway, resplendent with stone pillars.

A wide track now leads ssE beside a high stone boundary wall, and along this traverse there are some fine views down to your R back along the valley towards Bakewell, cradled within low-lying hills. The bridleway then descends to pass below more mature trees, mainly larch, where the steeper way down becomes slippery when wet. The pine needles change to broad leaves further down as beech, oak and a variety of other bird-friendly deciduous trees displace the less hospitable conifers. Continue downhill along the bridleway, disregarding all tree-harvesting tracks leading off into the woodland. Further down, this entails veering R to follow the way indicated by blue arrowhead markers.

The descent steepens as it winds out of the wooded area, and at the junction of ways below – an area often churned up and muddy from the movement of tractors – avoid the way leading off acutely to the R but do bear slightly R ahead to follow the continuation of the bridleway, which traverses around the hillside further on. This leads off initially towards the w, and is quite often muddy. Turn R when you reach the next fork along the bridleway signed

Gaining height above Bakewell.

129

*The pool near
Calton Pastures.*

to 'Bakewell', to head w. Pass by a private road leading off on the L
to Bowling Green Farm as you continue downhill along the signed
bridleway, which further on leads straight ahead as the shared farm
track turns R.

Pass through a swing gate and then bear R to walk beside the
iron railings marking the boundary of the grounds of Haddon Hall.
The obvious continuation way passes through three more gates,
the last one of which provides entry to a surfaced farm access
lane. Turn L and follow the lane down as it curves beside a continuation of the boundary fence, still on your immediate L. The River
Wye then appears, and just before reaching it the path continuing
towards Bakewell leads off to the R. However, to visit Haddon Hall
turn the opposite way, L, about 20 paces further on and follow the
narrow path downstream to reach the main A6(T) road (Haddon
Road) a short distance further on. Turn L and walk to the entrance
gates of Haddon Hall, which are just off this road.

Afterwards, walk back along the course of the River Wye and
turn L at MR 229½670½, visited for the second time, to continue
directly towards Bakewell. This turning is signed 'Public bridleway
to Coombs Road'. The way follows the meanders of the River Wye
upstream; keep to the lower ground on this final section and avoid
being led uphill by a path heading into the woodland. Further on,
pass through a gap in the fence ahead (where it is often muddy)
and then cross over a ditch on your L using a waysigned bridge.
From here, head towards the now visible church spire in Bakewell
and, keeping a hedge to your R, cross over the s-stile in the fence
ahead, pass through swing gates positioned at the far end of the
adjacent meadow, and cover the short remaining distance back to
the carpark.

TACKLING THE WALK

CASUAL WALKERS

This walk is perfect for walkers who do not want anything too strenuous and wish to spend some time exploring Haddon Hall and its grounds.

FAMILY WALKERS

The walk is also well suited to family groups. The higher ground of Calton Pastures may be avoided by keeping to the woodland paths which lead E, to connect with the described route at MR 244673½.

STRONG, EXPERIENCED WALKERS

This walk is neither long nor strenuous, and if you have more than half a day at your disposal the route may be extended conveniently by walking to Edensor – and perhaps even Chatsworth – and back.

PLACES OF INTEREST

BAKEWELL

An attractive tourist centre, Bakewell is all hustle and bustle on Mondays, which is market day. The town is known nationally for its Bakewell tart or pudding, said to have been discovered accidentally by a local cook. The River Wye flows majestically through the town and there is a recreation area and duck-feeding space along the riverside walkway, which is always open. The headquarters of the Peak National Park Authority are situated at Aldern House on a hillside overlooking the town, just off the Baslow Road.

HADDON HALL

The Derbyshire seat of the Duke of Rutland, Haddon Hall is promoted as England's most romantic and unspoilt medieval and Tudor house. A major tourist attraction, Haddon Hall contains a fourteenth-century chapel, its walls adorned with fine frescos. With roses in abundance, the award-winning gardens will delight all who wander around, being the epitome of an 'English country garden'.

A licensed restaurant is situated in the seventeenth-century stable block and there is a gift shop near the gatehouse. Unfortunately, because of its distance from the carpark and the steep approach to its entrance, Haddon Hall is not entirely suitable for either the elderly or disabled, but all are very welcome.

18 OVER HADDON, BRADFORD DALE AND LATHKILL DALE

STARTING/ FINISHING POINT
Carpark at Over Haddon OLM 24: MR 203664

GRADING OF WALK
Easy/straight-forward

TIME ALLOWANCE
3½ hours

DISTANCE
9.1km (5.7 miles)

TOTAL HEIGHT GAINED
280m (920ft)

HIGHEST POINT
Above Youlgreave 267m (875ft)

GRADIENTS
Some short, steep ups and downs, but no real challenges.

PARKING
Large, well-appointed, split-level carpark holds up to 50 cars but is very popular – and expensive.

PUBLIC TRANSPORT
None.

OVERVIEW/INTEREST
Explore tranquil Bradford Dale and Lathkill Dale. Magnificent limestone cliffs and other rock features. Section of the route across rural country-side. Superb views throughout. Extensive fauna and flora, including a nature reserve.

AMENITIES
Toilet facilities at the carpark. Refreshments available from cafés and the Lathkill Hotel at Over Haddon. There are more of these facilities at Youlgreave, at Meadow Cottage tea room and the George Hotel.

FOOTPATHS AND WAYSIGNS
Paths are clear and very well maintained for most of the way. Some less clearly defined grassy paths across rural countryside. Very few boggy areas and virtually no erosion. Waysigns are adequate to very helpful.

TURN R out of the carpark beside the toilet block and head steeply downhill, passing the Yew Tree tea room on your L to reach the tiny St Anne's Church, also on your L. The magnificent stone for this was quarried from Magpie Mine at nearby Sheldon Moor. This beautifully proportioned building is well worth a visit and from the memorial seat in its grounds there are splendid views down towards Lathkill Dale, towards which you are heading. Follow the twisting, narrow lane down, disregarding a signed footpath off to your L, to reach the bottom of the steep-sided, densely

132

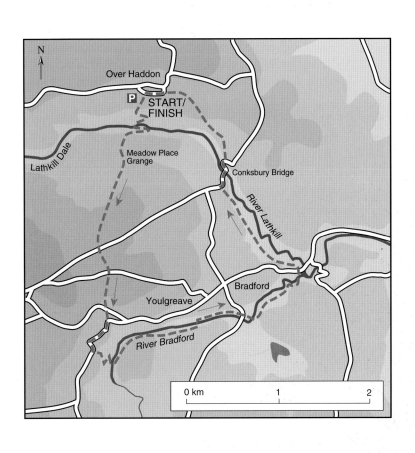

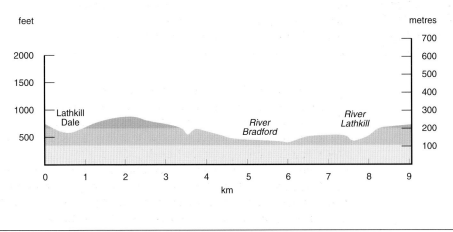

wooded, limestone dale at Lathkill Lodge. As you descend, the overhead foliage is provided by an attractive mixture of beech, hazel and sycamore trees.

Cross the footpath along the N bank of the River Lathkill and then cross over the river via the ancient stone footbridge. Turn L to continue up the wide track, which is surfaced with compacted earth and stones. This leads along a straightish diagonal and then bends acutely to the R as it climbs up out of the confined dale along a second straight traverse. Pass through the wooden gate at

the top where there are fine open views, particularly to the N back across Lathkill Dale towards Over Haddon. Turn L as indicated by the waysign, to walk slightly downhill across the adjacent field towards the farm buildings of Meadow Place Grange.

Enter and leave the farm through metal gates, keeping to the public footpath which is signed to 'Youlgreave and Middleton'. Beyond a third gate and w-stile, the continuation route funnels uphill between converging stone walls and, after passing a spreading chestnut tree, you will pass through a final gateway to gain

Walkers beside the River Bradford approaching Alport.

access to the open countryside ahead. Be careful now to fork R, following the public footpath signed to 'Middleton (Moor Lane)' and disregarding the alternative path on the L which leads to Youlgreave. The way continues to rise, initially beside a continuation of the stone walling. However, within a short distance you should bear L away from the line of this wall, to follow a less well-defined path which is again signed to 'Moor Lane'.

You are now walking SSW up towards the brow of the grassy hillock straight ahead. Keep to this bearing as the waysigned path crosses in sequence a W-stile, a large meadow, another W-stile, another large field and a final W-stile, which provides access to Back Lane at MR 198648. Cross the lane and exit via a further W-stile to continue along the signed footpath, now walking slightly downhill towards a gap in the narrow strip of trees directly ahead. Use the stiles to pass conveniently through this gap as the way continues SE and across a field to reach a second minor road (Moor Lane) at a metal gateway. Cross over the road to leave it through another G-stile, this one adjacent to a wooden gate. From here, the path leads slightly downhill beside a stone wall on your L, heading S towards tree-fringed Bradford Dale, now in view below.

The route then passes through a series of enclosed, narrow fields, and you will use more G-stiles and redundant gateways to pass through the stone boundary walls of these as you progressively lose height. On this relatively complicated section, keep near to the intermittent dry stone walling on your L without ever crossing it. You will reach another road, where you are informed that you have been heading from Over Haddon! Take care crossing this, as visibility along it is restricted by bends. Proceed further downhill along the footpath indicated by a white arrowhead bearing the number 3. This path is accessed over yet another W-stile and the subsequent descent is steeper than before, along a well-used path which serves several different walking routes.

You will reach a final road at a gateway and, after passing through the G-stile, cross over and then turn R and walk along the road using the narrow pavement on the far side (you are now keeping company with local walk 3 and also part of the Limestone Way). Follow the road for about 400 paces to reach a severe hairpin bend to the L. Immediately after this, branch off L along a narrow, rough path that descends quite steeply through overgrown thickets down the R flank of a steep side valley that connects with Bradford Dale to the SE. Keep an eye on young children during this descent, because there are loose stones underfoot and a steep drop to your L. The final part of the way down curves around to the R, before tracking back L to reveal tantalizing glimpses of wooded Bradford Dale below.

When you reach the floor of the dale, cross the River Bradford via the ancient arched stone bridge and then turn L to continue along this superb valley, still in company with walk 3 and the Limestone Way. A sublime 2.5km (1½ mile) stretch follows as the densely wooded dale threads below the villages of Youlgreave and Bradford, the clear, cool waters of the River Bradford flowing through and down a succession of catchment pools held back by low retaining weirs. There is much activity from fish and birds in, on and above these tranquil waters, which are also rich in plant life. The sounds of fish splashing, birds singing, the odd scurrying of woodland animals seeking better cover and the crunching of your boots is all that disturbs the utter peace and silence of this pleasant dale.

Partway along this stretch you will cross the River Bradford at MR 209640 by means of a raised stone footbridge. Just above this crossing there is an opportunity to sample delicious refreshments at the attractively located Meadow Cottage, with its splendid tea gardens and 'Teas with Hovis' sign from a bygone era. Afterwards, continue down the widening dale by passing through a swing gate. The path leads E along an obvious way, passing below the buildings of first Youlgreave and then Bradford, both above on your L. The route downstream leads to a G-stile at two wooden gates, and this provides entry to the surfaced lane beyond. Ignore the way off to your R over the footbridge and instead walk about 30

A refreshment sign points towards lower Bradford Dale.

paces straight ahead, then cross another lane before using a wide gateway to continue along the signed public footpath. The path curves to the L to pass below limestone cliffs, at the second of which an all-weather seat has been thoughtfully positioned below the protruding rock.

Do not cross over the arched stone bridge virtually opposite the seat, but continue along the dale using the tracks and, where possible, grassy short-cuts to make good progress NW along Lathkill Dale. Wild flowers abound along this stretch during the summer months, competing for the confined space with hawthorn, nettles and thistles. Always keep along the bottom of the dale, and further on use a G-stile or K-gate to escape from the surfaced way as this climbs uphill away from the river. You will then pass another quite spectacular limestone cliff and a short distance away, after passing through another G-stile at a white-painted gate, you will reach the road through Alport at another such gate. Cross the road and leave through the G-stile opposite to continue along Lathkill Dale, walking NW in the direction signed to 'Conksbury', veering R away from the farm track to do so.

The obvious continuation way leads further upstream along the L bank of the river, passing through a succession of G-stiles – nine in all. During this section along the edge of meadowland the route crosses a bridleway leading to Haddon Hall, which you should disregard. Following this, the continuation route winds gently uphill beside a wooded area, to pass through two more G-stiles before leading you to the minor road just above Conksbury Bridge. Turn R down the road and cross the attractive triple-arched stone bridge, taking care with competing vehicles on the narrow crossing. Keep to the surfaced roadway as it climbs out of the dale, ignoring the continuation waysigned path which hugs the bottom of the dale. However, when the road bends sharply to the R you should turn off L, passing through the parking layby to use a G-stile into the rough, stony path which climbs up the slope ahead to the R.

This leads to a very narrow G-stile, and above this minor challenge the narrow but clearly defined path leads further uphill to reach flatter, grassy ground above. Continue along the path leading N and then NW along the top of Lathkill Dale, passing enclosed woodland on your L and heading back towards the buildings of Over Haddon, which are now in sight again. The way there passes through another collection of G- and S-stiles, which will temporarily hinder your progress. This is fortunate, because when the weather is kind the views from here both W along Lathkill Dale and back towards Youlgreave are stunning.

A well-used, obvious diagonal path leads back towards Over Haddon, and during this approach you will need to bear R over a

P-stile to walk away from the dale and more directly towards the outlying buildings of the village, heading NW. There is another stile combination to negotiate before you reach Over Haddon at its E tip, courtesy of yet another G-stile. Walk L down the road, passing in front of (or through) the Lathkill Hotel. Then fork R, keeping to the higher ground to walk through the attractive elongated village, heading W and veering L at the Lathkill Dale Craft Centre, which is well worth a visit. Walk past the War Memorial to reach the road junction with its grass triangle, near to which the walk started. The carpark is on the far side.

TACKLING THE WALK

CASUAL WALKERS

This short walk is ideal for casual walkers, with continual interest and the ups and downs well spaced out, and even then not too strenuous.

FAMILY WALKERS

This walk should also appeal to family groups. The relatively severe descent into Bradford Dale may be avoided by turning L along the road, walking into Youlgreave and then returning to the described route at MR 209640.

STRONG, EXPERIENCED WALKERS

This short route is full of interest and might appeal as a pleasant evening stroll during the height of summer. The route is easily extended in a variety of ways, and places such as Haddon Hall or the full length of Lathkill Dale could be included in a more challenging extension of your own choice.

PLACES OF INTEREST

BRADFORD DALE AND LATHKILL DALE

The interconnected dales of Bradford and Lathkill must represent some of the finest limestone scenery to be seen anywhere. They certainly rank as two of my favourite places in the whole of the White Peak. The two dales, a delightful mix of placid waters, craggy limestone outcrops, ancient woodland and green pastures, support a great variety of flora and fauna. There is a National Nature Reserve in Lathkill Dale.

139

19 HARTINGTON, BIGGIN DALE, WOLFSCOTE DALE AND BERESFORD DALE

**STARTING/
FINISHING POINT**
Carpark at
Hartington OLM 24:
127603

**GRADING
OF WALK**
Easy/straight-
forward

**TIME
ALLOWANCE**
3½ hours

DISTANCE
9.3km (5.8 miles)

**TOTAL HEIGHT
GAINED**
120m (395ft)

HIGHEST POINT
Highfield Lane 317m
(1040 ft)

GRADIENTS
No steep or difficult gradients.

PARKING
Large carpark holds over 50 cars. Additional parking in the village.

PUBLIC TRANSPORT
Bus routes 57, 181, 202, 420, 441, 442, 446, 456, 464 and 901.

OVERVIEW/INTEREST
Starts from the attractive village of Hartington. Open landscapes with distant views near start and finish. Superb interconnected limestone dales with fascinating rock features. Includes a section along the meandering River Dove.

AMENITIES
Toilets opposite the carpark. Refreshment facilities in Hartington range from cafés to comfortable hotels.

FOOTPATHS AND WAYSIGNS
Paths are generally good, with those along the dales excellent. Several muddy areas after heavy rain and occasional rougher, stony ground. Signs are more than adequate in most places.

TURN L from the carpark and walk back through the village, following the main road as it bends to the R at the central triangle. Turn R along the lane signed 'Youth hostel 250yd' and walk uphill to reach this establishment. As you gain height there are good views down across the meadows below towards St Giles' Church. Go past the first narrow lane on your R, continuing straight ahead to reach the quite splendidly positioned youth hostel. Disregard the walled track leading off directly opposite the hostel and then about 60 paces further on, just past the speed derestriction road sign, turn R through a metal gate to access the signed public footpath. Wide-ranging views appear from here

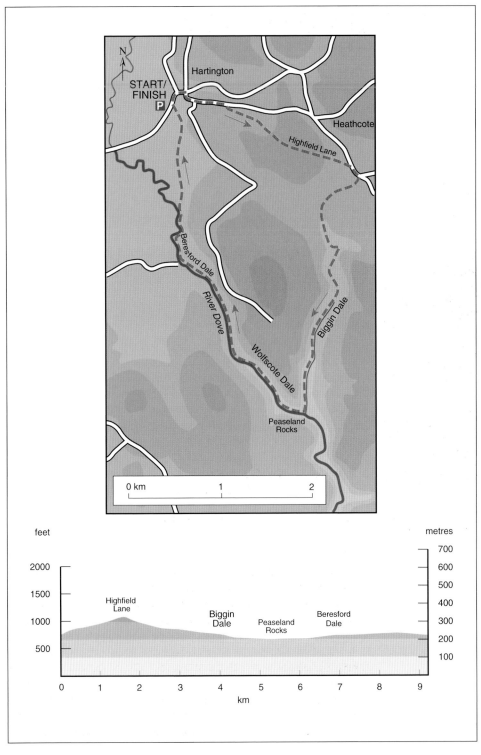

N

Hartington

START/
FINISH
P

Heathcote

Highfield Lane

Beresford Dale

River Dove

Biggin Dale

Wolfscote Dale

Peaseland
Rocks

| 0 km | 1 | 2 |

feet

metres

700
600
500
400
2000
300
1500
Highfield
Lane
Biggin
Dale
Beresford
Dale
200
1000
Peaseland
Rocks
500
100

0   1   2   3   4   5   6   7   8   9
km

The rural scene surrounding Heathcote.

of pleasant, undulating, hilly countryside liberally covered with copses of trees and orderly, walled pastures.

Cross the adjacent field heading for a gate ahead and maintain this diagonal, bearing slightly L across the corner of the next field, to locate and use a W-stile at which another footpath sign has been placed. This provides entry to the walled track named Highfield Lane along which you should veer R. The continuation way winds SE over the brow of the hill ahead, passing a stone barn, to lead you to Dale End below, less than 2km (1¼ miles) away. During your descent, the scar of Biggin Dale – part of your continuation route – comes into view over to your R, to the SSE. Along here, the buildings of Heathcote may also be positioned in the NE, to your L. The village of Biggin lies directly ahead.

Ignoring a way off to your R, follow the walled track past Dale End House to reach a surfaced lane. Turn R along this and within a further 100 paces turn R again to continue along the signed public footpath leading down into Biggin Dale. This is entered through a narrow G-stile and an English Nature sign welcomes you to the dale, which is under their care. The way then threads southwards, following the folds and grassy contortions of the tranquil dale downhill. Continue along the obvious wide path which hugs the bottom of the dale as the surrounding scenery becomes increasingly spectacular, with the rounded, grassy slopes of the upper valley surrendering to craggy limestone cliffs and rocky outcrops lower down.

142

For most of its length Biggin Dale is a dry dale, but a small watercourse does appear for part of the way further down and for some distance it competes for space with your path. Before you reach this section, use an S-stile to cross over the dry stone walling that blocks your progress, and further down disregard the public bridleway to Hartington which branches off uphill to your R. The path leads to an intersection of ways and your continuation route follows Biggin Dale around to the R, on the far side of a limestone wall ahead. To reach this, first bear L to circle around a dew pond, using a wooden gate above on the L to pass through another dry stone wall, then turn immediately R to continue along the signed public bridleway, which can be very muddy.

The sides of the dale continue to steepen and the plunging slopes become covered with large patches of gorse intermingled with areas of limestone scree. Then, past another wooden gate, hawthorn shrubs and willow add their presence. This section can become wet underfoot. Beyond a redundant gateway, the lower reaches of Biggin Dale become even more spectacular as vertical limestone cliffs interspersed with steep slopes of scree form the sides of the dale. This fascinating scenery still surrounds you as you reach the junction with Wolfscote Dale at the spectacular vertical towers and cliffs of Peaseland Rocks, at MR 142569½. Here you make contact with some proper water in the form of the River Dove. Turn R to follow this impatient, gurgling river upstream, where the delights of Wolfscote and Beresford Dales await you. Pedestrian traffic flow also increases along these two popular dales.

Spectacular scenery continues as you follow the obvious, wide and well-drained path, which leads NW along the sheltered dale beneath more vertical walls of pearly-white limestone. Watch out along here for unstable scree, which in places even intrudes on to your pathway. Further up, the features of Wolfscote Dale become progressively less dramatic as the sides of the dale change to lower, more rounded and less steep, grassy slopes. A stile and adjacent wooden gate signal that you are approaching the N reaches of the dale, and a short distance beyond these features and past more limestone cliffs and screes you will emerge from the jaws of the valley.

Here you should avoid crossing over the River Dove and also veering off to the R uphill along a walled track. Instead, pass through two G-stiles and then cross the flat, private meadowland directly ahead by means of a continuation of the public right of way. Your heading remains to the N across the low-lying ground, which is often boggy. Head around to the R, searching out the slightly higher ground when the going is particularly bad. The crossing leads towards Beresford Dale directly ahead and the exit from the meadow is through an unusually shaped stone G-stile. After this, cross the River Dove via the adjacent bridge and turn R to continue along the path signed to 'Hartington', which threads through Beresford Dale *en route*.

Beresford Dale is a much shorter, less spectacular valley than either of the two previous ones, but it is nevertheless interesting and has a tranquil charm of its own as the River Dove flows serenely and placidly through steep, wooded slopes of modest height, tumbling down a succession of weirs in the process. You will re-cross the river and a short distance further on the route emerges from the dale to commence a gradual ascent across more open countryside back towards Hartington. The clearly defined and well-trodden way leads through a gated G-stile positioned in a dry stone wall and then uphill, veering to the L of a grassy knoll, where you are requested to keep to the marked path.

Follow the waysigned route as it bears L towards the buildings of Hartington, which now come into view ahead. Cross a shallow, grassy depression then negotiate a G-stile and a wide gap in a stone wall, before the path bears R uphill to round another grassy hillock. The way then crosses a walled track flanked by W-stiles, which you

Peaseland Rocks in Wolfscote Dale.

use to continue along the final approach path into Hartington. This is again signed and it runs along adjacent to a limestone wall on your L. The path then descends through a gateway to lead you back to the road through the village. This is almost directly opposite the carpark, which you reach by striking a diagonal to your L.

TACKLING THE WALK

CASUAL WALKERS
This walk should appeal to all who enjoy a not too strenuous route through quite spectacular limestone scenery.

FAMILY WALKERS
Similar remarks apply to family groups and in fine weather you could make a full day of it, taking a picnic and finding a safe spot for the children to play by the side of the River Dove.

STRONG, EXPERIENCED WALKERS
This is a pleasant short stroll, involving little real effort. However, this can be remedied by extending the walk southwards through Mill Dale into Dove Dale and then circling back via Alstonefield.

PLACES OF INTEREST

HARTINGTON
Hartington first became a market town in 1203. Nowadays, a charming assortment of limestone-built dwellings, hotels, cafés and a few shops form the village, which is ideally situated for exploring the network of dales to the S. There has been a church in the village since Anglo-Saxon times and the foundations of the present towered building, St Giles' Church, were laid in the early thirteenth century. Since then the church and the churchyard have had a colourful and interesting history (literature in the church) and there is a most remarkable memorial to local man, Thomas Mellor, who lived to be 103.

BIGGIN DALE, WOLFSCOTE DALE AND BERESFORD DALE
These are three interconnected dales which conveniently provide a circular walk from Hartington to the N through the most spectacular limestone country. The powerful River Dove flows through Beresford and Wolfscote Dale and then continues S along Mill Dale and Dove Dale to pass between the villages of Ilam and Thorpe. Part of Biggin Dale is a National Nature Reserve where wild flowers attract a multitude of butterflies and other insects. There is also unusual gorse scrub in Biggin Dale which is rare in other limestone dales.

145

20 ALSTONEFIELD, STANSHOPE, HALL DALE, DOVE DALE AND MILL DALE

STARTING/ FINISHING POINT
Carpark at Alstonefield OLM 24: MR 131556

GRADING OF WALK
Moderate/ challenging

TIME ALLOWANCE
4 hours

DISTANCE
9.2km (5.7 miles)

TOTAL HEIGHT GAINED
180m (590ft)

HIGHEST POINT
Around Alstonefield 285m (935ft)

GRADIENTS
Some quite steep ups and downs, but these are well spaced out and not too demanding when taken at a comfortable pace.

PARKING
Tiny carpark holds up to 12 cars, with some space for coaches.

PUBLIC TRANSPORT
Bus routes 57A, 202, 441, 442 and 450.

OVERVIEW/INTEREST
Delightful start from the attractive hamlet of Alstonefield. Open scenery along the section to Mill Dale. Spectacular limestone scenery along the dales with cliffs, columns and caves. Enjoy the serenity of the River Dove flowing through a wooded gorge. Plenty of bird and animal wildlife.

AMENITIES
Toilets at the carpark. Refreshments available in Alstonefield at the George Inn and elsewhere. Further toilets at Milldale, plus a National Trust Information Barn and a shop selling ice cream, drinks etc.

FOOTPATHS AND WAYSIGNS
With few exceptions, paths range from good to first class. Some rougher ground, and several steeper downhill slopes become slippery when wet. Some waterlogged areas after heavy rain. Signs are adequate and route finding is not demanding.

TURN R out of the carpark and walk diagonally R across the adjacent coach-parking area to exit via a wide path leading slightly uphill, walking SW. Bear R along the road ahead to pass by a grass triangle. Veer R at the next road junction to pass another such triangle, this one on your R. Then turn L along the lane signed to 'Wetton 1¾: Ilam 3½: Dovedale 4½', before branching immediately L along an obscurely signed footpath. This is a broad, enclosed track which leads S between dry stone walling. The square-towered

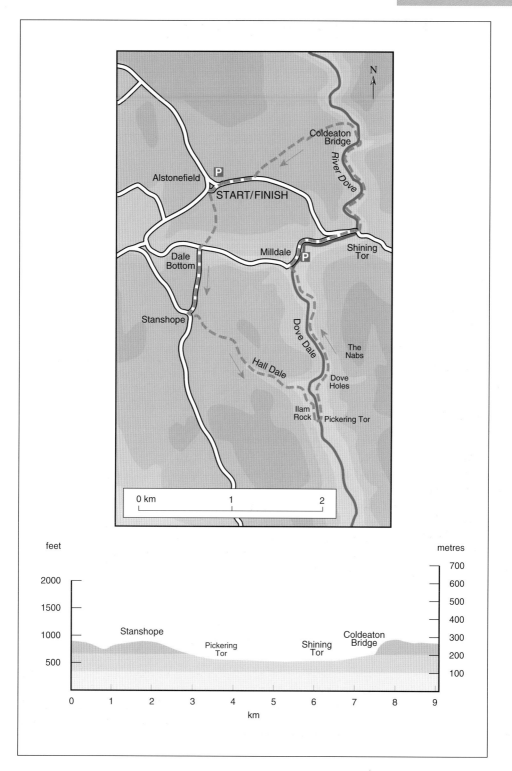

feet

Stanshope

Pickering
Tor

Shining
Tor

Coldeaton
Bridge

2000

1500

1000

500

0   1   2   3   4   5   6   7   8   9
km

metres

700
600
500
400
300
200
100

147

Alstonefield church will immediately come into view across the fields to your L. When the track bends sharply to the R, continue straight on, passing through a G-stile to the L of a wooden gate. The continuation way is down a gently sloping meadow next to a dry stone wall on your R.

Open views now appear ahead, further S, of low-lying, rounded hillsides consisting mainly of sheep pastures. The route passes close by a solitary mature tree, and after this you should veer R along a narrowing, grassy funnel. Go through a G-stile near a gateway, before the path leads sharply downhill along an eroded section which unfortunately becomes slippery in wet conditions. This descent leads to Dale Bottom, where you pass through a G-stile as a preliminary to crossing the lane. Depart uphill along the obvious continuation way, which leads further S. This wide, enclosed track leads equally steeply back uphill, and the height previously surrendered is quickly regained. There is a lovely cottage in Dale Bottom near to your crossing, the garden of which is a mass of white in February when the snowdrops are in flower. Later on in summer the blues, purples, magentas and oranges of lupins take over from the yellows of the daffodils which have flowered in between.

Eventually the steep gradient eases off and at the top of the brow you should turn around to spot Wetton Hill to the NW and Alstonefield church to the NNE. The passing of a barn signals that the climbing is all but over for the time being and that a straightforward, level stretch lies ahead. However, there is usually plenty of mud along here in heavy winter conditions – and sometimes in wet summers as well! The walled way winds around Grove Farm and then Church Farm as it approaches Stanshope; along here, you should ignore a footpath leading off to the R. When you reach the grass triangle, turn L and continue bearing L down the wide, walled path which tracks E towards Hall Dale. However, within a further 100 paces you should turn off R over a W-stile on to the footpath signed to 'Dovedale'.

From here, head across the corner of the adjacent field, veering L towards the nick of Hall Dale and the signed stone S-stile across the wall ahead. Over this, cross the corner of the next field to use another stile, having changed your direction slightly to SSW to head directly towards Hall Dale. An obvious continuation way now funnels more steeply into the recesses of the dale along a clearly waysigned route. Avoid using the next stile and footpath leading off on the R and continue downhill over gently sloping, grassy ground. Past the next two W-stiles the character of Hall Dale changes abruptly as steep, rocky slopes containing limestone buttresses and loose scree replace the gentler, undulating green meadowlands above.

From here, a quite delightful way threads through the interlacing sides of the steepening dry dale as you continue E towards Dove Dale, still some distance below. Cross over another stile, ignoring a side path on the R leading towards Bunster Hill. Continue along Hall Dale, where lower down the surface becomes rougher underfoot and loose stones and slippery sections force you to pay full attention to each step. After another w-stile, parts of Dove Dale around the jagged hill named The Nabs will come into view, and soon after this you will be standing on flat, grassy ground at the meeting of the two dales.

When you reach the River Dove, turn R to pass through a w-stile and continue S to reach and cross the footbridge spanning the river near to Ilam Rock and Pickering Tor. With its superb limestone columns, dark caves and meandering stream, this is a quite delightful spot. Turn L on the far side to head upstream back along Dove Dale, continuing N up the beautiful wooded dale. You will pass the jaws of Hall Dale once again and beyond this reach and then pass the caves of Dove Holes, above to your R. These are worth an inspection but be careful getting up and down because the polished, limestone rock is slippery!

Looking back towards Alstonefield church.

149

*The author at
Ilam Rock and
Pickering Tor,
Dove Dale.*

Beyond the caves, bear around to the L disregarding the path off on the R signed to 'Alsop-en-le-Dale'. Cross over another stile to walk past superb limestone tors that tumble down into the dale ahead. After you have climbed over a second stile the dale becomes less rugged, with rounded, interlocking grassy slopes replacing the more spectacular limestone tors and columns. More stiles and gates, including a spring-loaded one, follow before the path leads into the attractive hamlet of Milldale. You will enter this over Viator's Bridge, a venerable stone pack-horse crossing of the River Dove.

Walk past the entrance to the footpath leading off L by the side of Old Miller's Cottage and then bear R at the loop in the road ahead to continue walking N along Mill Dale. Here, make whatever use you can of the extended footpath beside the lane, before you are forced on to the surfaced way. The lane leads to Lode Mill where you should turn R at the T-junction, cross the River Dove again by means of the road bridge and then turn immediately L to descend down steps and rejoin the continuation footpath signed to 'Beresford Dale:Wolfscote Dale: Hartington'. The limestone cliff now rising steeply behind you is Shining Tor. Through the twin G-stiles situated at Fishpond Bank the path meanders N, following the broad sweeps of the river as it flows majestically through the steep-sided dale.

Keep on along the bottom of the valley as more G-stiles come and go, avoiding crossing either of the two footbridges across the river, both signed 'Private'. The path continues up the rising dale passing limestone outcrops, areas of gorse and a series of miniature weirs or tiny waterfalls. This flat section of the route continues to Coldeaton Bridge, where you will use another G-stile and gate combination.Then, just beyond an isolated stone building, you should turn L over the footbridge spanning the River Dove, crossing this for the last time on the walk.

A narrow but well-used path winds steeply up the far grassy slope to reach the rim of the dale high above. Follow this path through a shallow hollow, where its surface changes to fragments of rock and loose stones.The way leads to the top of Gipsy Bank (where there is a National Trust sign) and you should cross over a stile to continue SW along the waysigned, walled path. A clear, obvious path then leads gently on up the slope beside a hedge of hawthorn trees. Following a kink to the R, the (often muddy) way connects at a T-junction with the road ahead.Turn R and use the road to walk back into Alstonefield.Turn L when you reach the first grass triangle and pass by (or via) the George Inn at a second triangle, which sports a gnarled sycamore tree. Veer R to pass by Jean Goodwin Cottage Studio and the post office.Turn R again when you reach the next grass triangle and the path opposite will lead you back to the carpark.

TACKLING THE WALK

CASUAL WALKERS
This is good, challenging route that is full of interest and should give great satisfaction on completion.

FAMILY WALKERS
The walk is also suitable for families with older children. Those with younger offspring could cut out the final, fairly exacting loop of the route by returning directly to Alstonefield from Milldale along Millway Lane.

STRONG, EXPERIENCED WALKERS
This reasonably strenuous and interesting short walk could occupy a full half day if it is extended further down Dove Dale and/or into Wolfscote Dale.

PLACES OF INTEREST

ALSTONEFIELD

For walkers, Alstonefield – the village of grass triangles – can be quite exasperating to get out of, and when this is achieved the most difficult bit of route finding for the whole day is usually over! Although of former importance, the tiny village is today an unspoilt, rustic backwater and its two principal buildings are its church, a fine multi-styled building, and the George Inn, where delicious home-cooked food is available.

HALL DALE, DOVE DALE AND MILL DALE

Hall Dale differs from the interconnected Dove Dale and Mill Dale in a number of respects. Hall Dale is a dry dale, whereas the River Dove flows majestically along the other two: in addition, Hall Dale winds fairly steeply downhill whereas the valley floors of Dove Dale and Mill Dale are almost flat. However, one attribute which all three dales share is their spectacular limestone scenery. A fascinating mixture of cliffs, crags, scree, tors, columns and steep, grassy slopes, they make superb walking terrain for all who wish to explore the White Peak on foot.

USEFUL ADDRESSES
AND PUBLICATIONS

THE useful addresses and telephone numbers listed here are arranged in two sections. The first covers places of interest mentioned in association with the walks and other useful contacts, given in walk sequence. The second lists other relevant organizations, presented in alphabetical order.

USEFUL ADDRESSES

WALK 1

Cycle Hire Centre
Fairholmes
Derwent
Sheffield S30 2AQ
Tel: 01433 651261

Upper Derwent Valley:

Severn Trent Water
Matlock
Tel: 01629 55051

National Trust
Hope Valley
Tel: 01433 70368

Forestry Commission
Hope Valley
Tel: 01433 50072

Peak National Park
Bakewell
Tel: 01629 814321

Public Rights of Way Information
Tel: 01742 734448/01629 580000

Fairholmes Information Centre
Tel: 01433 650953

WALK 3

Edale Cottage Café
Station Approach
Edale
Hope Valley S30 2ZA
Tel: 01433 670293

WALK 4

Blue John Cavern and Mine
Castleton
via Sheffield S30 2WP
Tel: 01433 620638

Treak Cliff Cavern
Castleton
via Sheffield S30 2WP
Tel: 01433 620571

WALK 7

The National Trust
Lyme Park, Disley
Stockport SK12 2NX
Tel: 01663 762023

WALK 8

Goyt Valley:

Local Forestry Commission
Tel: 01433 50072

Local North West Water
Tel: 01457 869133

Local Peak Park Planning Board
Tel: 01629 814321

WALK 9

Cheshire Wildlife Trust
Grebe House
Rease Heath
Nantwich
Cheshire
Tel: 01270 610180

WALK 12

Castleton Tourist Office
Castle Street
Castleton
via Sheffield S30 2WG
Tel: 01433 620679/01629 813227

The Custodian
Peak Cavern
Castleton
via Sheffield S30 2WS
Tel: 01433 20285

English Heritage
Peveril Castle
Castleton
via Sheffield
Tel: 01433 620613

Speedwell Cavern Ltd
Winnats Pass
Castleton
via Sheffield S30 2WA
Tel: 01433 620512

WALK 14

Cathedral of The Peak Flower Festival
Tideswell Parish Church
Tideswell
Nr Buxton
Derbyshire
Tel: 01298 872266 (Mrs A. Hopkins)

WALK 15

Monsal Head and Trail:

Busline enquiry service
Tel: 01332 292200

Information Centres:
Buxton: Tel: 01298 251106
Bakewell: Tel: 01629 813227
Matlock: Tel: 01629 55082

WALK 16

Chatsworth House
Chatsworth
Bakewell
Derbyshire DE45 1PP
Tel: 01246 582204

WALK 17

Haddon Hall
Bakewell
Derbyshire DE45 1LA
Tel: 01629 812855

WALK 18

Lathkill Dale Visitor Information Centre,
    National Nature Reserve and Craft Centre
The Site Manager, English Nature
Over Haddon
Bakewell
Derbyshire DE45 1JE
Tel: 01629 815095

Meadow Cottage Tea Room
Holywell Lane, Youlgreave
Nr Bakewell
Derbyshire DE45 1UT
Tel: 01629 636523

WALK 20

The George Inn
Alstonefield
Nr Ashbourne
Derbyshire DE6 2FX
Tel: 01335 310205

OTHER RELEVANT ORGANIZATIONS

Council for the Protection of Rural England
(CPRE)
Sheffield and Peak Branch
22 Endcliffe Crescent
Ranmoor
Sheffield S10 3EF
Tel: 01742 665822

Derbyshire County Council Planning
Department
County Offices
Matlock
Derbyshire DE4 3AG
Tel: 01629 580000

East Midlands Tourist Board
Exchequergate
Lincoln LN2 1PZ
Tel: 01522 531521

English Heritage (East Midlands & East Anglia)
Hazelrigg House
33 Marefair
Northampton NN1 1SR
Tel: 01604 730350

English Nature (Peak & Derbyshire Region)
Manor Barn
Over Haddon
Bakewell
Derbyshire DE4S 1JE
Tel: 01629 815095

Forestry Commission
Sherwood Forest Office
Forestry Enterprises
Edwinstowe
Mansfield
Nottinghamshire NG21 9JL
Tel: 01623 822447

Information Centres:

Bakewell
Tel: 01629 813227

Castleton
Tel: 01433 620679

Edale
Tel: 01433 670207

Fairholmes (Derwent Valley):
Tel: 01433 650953

The following are open weekends only and
do not have telephone facilities.

Hartington

Langsett (Nr Sheffield)

Torside (Longendale Valley)

Mobile Information Centre:

The Peak National Park Planning Board's
caravan will be at various summer events,
including well dressings.

National Trust (East Midlands Region)

The Stables
Clumber Park
Worksop
Nottinghamshire S80 3BE
Tel: 01909 486411

Peak National Park:

National Park Authority Office
Aldern House
Baslow Road
Bakewell
Derbyshire DE45 1AE
Tel: 01629 814321

Peak National Park Study Centre
Losehill Hall
Castleton
Sheffield S30 2WB
Tel: 01433 620373

Tourist Information Centres:

Ashbourne
Tel: 01335 343666

Buxton
Tel: 01298 25106

155

Glossop
Tel: 01457 855920

Holmfirth
Tel: 01484 687603

Leek
Tel: 01538 381000

Matlock
Tel: 01629 55082

WATER AUTHORITIES

North West Water
PO Box 30
New Town House
Buttermarket Street
Warrington
Cheshire WA1 2QG
Tel: 01629 825850

Severn Trent Water
Abelson House
Sheldon Road
Birmingham B26 3PR
Tel: 0121-722 4000

Yorkshire Water
West Riding House
Albion Street
Leeds LS1 5AA
Tel: 01532 448301

Youth Hostels Association
Central Regional Office
PO Box 11
Matlock
Derbyshire DE4 2XA
Tel: 01629 825850

**MOUNTAIN RESCUE SERVICE
999 EMERGENCY**

PUBLICATIONS

The Peak National Park Authority publish a comprehensive series of Educational Fact Sheets covering such subjects as the National Parks, Tourism, the Pennine Way, Land Use, Conservation, Design, Climate, Geology, Mining and Quarrying, Hill Farming, Employment, and data on several of the larger towns and villages. Copies of these Fact Sheets may be obtained from the Peak National Park Study Centre at Losehill Hall (see page 155). Other relevant publications include the informative free newspaper *Peakland Post*.

Also available is a modestly priced timetable covering both bus and train services operating within the Peak District. This is a particularly helpful publication: the information is clearly and comprehensively scheduled, and it forms part of the wider campaign by the National Park Authority and Derbyshire County Council to encourage greater awareness and use of public transport.

GLOSSARY

The following geological terms, dialect words and place names have been used in the book or may be met with by those undertaking the walks.

Blue John variety of fluorite, containing purple, yellow or colourless bands
booth herdsman's shelter or cowshed
cairn heap of stones, usually pointed
cavern large natural space or chamber underground
clough stream valley, narrow ravine
col sharp-edged or saddle-shaped pass
crag steep, rugged rock or peak
culvert drain or covered channel
dale valley
edge steep cliff
fault fracture in rocks, the opposite sides of which have been displaced relative to one another, either vertically or horizontally
ginnel narrow passageway between buildings
gorge deep, narrow, steep-walled valley
grit coarse-grained, sandy sediment
grough/hag natural channel or fissure in a peat moor; deep drainage ditch in a peat bog
hause summit of narrow pass or col
heath large, open area with scrubby vegetation, usually heathers
jagger leader of pack-horse train
knoll small, rounded hill
knott rocky outcrop
limestone sedimentary rock composed almost entirely of calcium carbonate, mainly as calcite
millstone-grit coarse-grained, carboniferous sandstone used for the manufacture of mill stones
nab/neb promontory
pike pointed summit
rigg ridge
rindle stream which flows only in wet weather
sandstone sedimentary rock of sand and/or silt bound together by a cement, often calcite or silica; quartz grains predominate in the average sandstone
scar escarpment
scree loose shattered rock on mountain slope
shale fine-grained sedimentary rock formed predominantly of compacted clay
sinkhole area, especially in limestone, where a surface stream sinks underground
slough hole where water collects; hollow filled with mud or bog
squeezer-stile stile containing a narrow gap
toadstone Derbyshire name for decomposed basaltic, volcanic rocks
tor core of unweathered, harder rocks standing above a surrounding area of weathered rock
tower tall, squarish structure of unweathered rock, usually located on or near steep slopes of rocky gorges
well spring or stream
well dressing custom of decorating wells with floral tributes in thanks for water

SUMMARY TABLE

WALK	DESCRIPTION	GRADING OF WALK Easy/ straightforward	Moderate/ challenging	TIME ALLOWANCE Hours	DISTANCE Km	Miles	TOTAL HEIGHT GAINED Metres	Feet	HIGHEST POINT Metres	Feet
	THE DARK PEAK									
1	Derwent Reservoir and the Upper Derwent Valley	✓		3	7.2	4.5	225	740	380	1245
2	Hayfield and Kinder Reservoir	✓		3½	7.4	4.6	210	690	350	1150
3	Edale, Grindsbrook and Grindslow Knoll		✓✓✓	4	6.9	4.3	420	1380	601	1970
4	Mam Tor and Hollins Cross (Caverns and Mines)		✓✓✓	3	5.8	3.6	270	875	517	1695
5	Hope and Win Hill		✓✓✓	4	9.3	5.8	300	985	462	1515
6	Higger Tor, Burbage Rocks and Carl Wark	✓		2½	5.8	3.6	185	605	434	1425
7	Lyme Park and Bow Stones	✓✓		4	9.2	5.7	210	690	390	1280
8	Pym Chair, Cats Tor, Shining Tor and Errwood Hall	✓✓	✓	4	9.4	5.9	350	1150	559	1835
9	Macclesfield Forest and Shutlingsloe		✓✓	3	6.2	3.8	250	820	506	1660
10	The Roaches, Lud's Church (Cave) and Hanging Stone		✓✓✓	5	11	6.9	350	1150	505	1655
11	Curbar Edge, Eagle Stone and Wellington's Monument	✓		2½	6.3	3.9	100	330	330	1085
	THE WHITE PEAK									
12	Castleton, Cave Dale and the Winnats Pass	✓✓		3½	7.4	4.6	270	885	470	1540
13	Miller's Dale, Chee Dale and Wormhill	✓✓		3	7.6	4.7	150	490	315	1035
14	Tideswell Dale, Miller's Dale, Cressbrook, Cressbrook Dale and Tansley Dale	✓✓	✓✓	3	8.2	5.1	160	525	300	985
15	Ashford in the Water, Monsal Head and Monsal Dale		✓✓	3½	8.9	5.5	230	755	265	870
16	Baslow and Chatsworth House and Park	✓		3	7.1	4.4	145	475	235	770
17	Bakewell and Haddon Hall	✓		4	9	5.6	235	770	285	935
18	Over Haddon, Bradford Dale and Lathkill Dale	✓		3½	9.1	5.7	280	920	267	875
19	Hartington, Biggin Dale, Wolfscote Dale and Beresford Dale	✓✓✓	.	3½	9.3	5.8	120	395	317	1040
20	Alstonefield, Stanshope, Hall Dale, Dove Dale and Mill Dale		✓	4	9.2	5.7	180	590	285	935

INDEX